Tales of A Five-Star Missionary

By Ellie Goolkasian Lugo

To Brenda and John, may God richly bless your lives!

Ellie Goolkasian Lugo

Dedication

This book is dedicated to my parents. Despite all my wanderings their love has never wavered. To Enrique, my amazing husband, who shows me daily how we should love in Christ. And to God, the Source of all love.

Acknowledgements

I thank God for those who make my life and ministry possible:

Dr. Arnie Gorske, a faithful and patient mentor who always seeks to do healthcare ministry in the most excellent way.

My precious friends and supporters who have prayed for, listened to, or housed me, donated to the ministry or been my friend – I could never express your significance.

Pastor Tom Theriault, the best missions pastor on the planet.

The people of the San Quintin Valley in Mexico, for modelling a humble and welcoming spirit to a five-star gringa.

Introduction

In the fall of 2007, as I packed up or sold all my belongings, most of the county was on fire. News clips showed homes in Poway and Scripps Ranch, mansions in Rancho Santa Fe, in flames. One million people had been evacuated and were seeking shelter.

"Have you been watching TV?" a friend asked. "It looks like something out of the *Left Behind* series!"

The sky over my neighborhood was a billowing gray-and-orange mass of residue and heat, leaving no doubt the inferno was both real and dangerously close.

"Do not try to sweep up the soot left by the fires! Inhaling these particles can cause toxic reactions."

Too late. I heard this warning broadcast *after* cleaning every cranny of my garage with a dust pan and brush. The announcer listed the possible symptoms, "general malaise, weakness, headache, vertigo," and I responded, "Yup! Yup! Yes! Uh huh, got 'em all!"

I had to keep working. My deadline to be out of the house was the next day, Tuesday. The orphanage expected me on Wednesday.

How had this happened?

Before Christ I had been an expert hedonist. Life was a buffet of endorphins – luxury vacations around the world, gourmet cooking and restaurants, running on the beach, love affairs, movies, books - even my career as an ICU nurse gave me an adrenaline high! Though I had been raised Catholic and never stopped believing in God, I put off making a commitment to Christ.

"If you died today, do you know if you'd go to heaven?" one of my best friends asked me.

Gary was a born-again Christian. We worked twelve-hour night shifts together and on rare slow nights, kept each other awake telling jokes.

"He's a strong Christian, but we have so much fun together!"

This was my explanation to people who wondered about our friendship; however, the truth went deeper. He was my brother-in-Christ before I'd ever heard the term; he loved me, listened to me, and did not judge, though some of my stories made him blush!

Christ used him to stir up long-buried truth in me. When some other friends invited me to attend an evangelical church in Oceanside, I went gladly, feeling a vague sense of relief. My hedonistic pursuits had never included praise songs or preaching, but how my weary soul exulted that day in worship!

"Have you made the world your god?" the pastor asked. "Do your cravings and desires, your pride, rule over you? Today is the day to talk to Jesus, tell Him you're sorry you've sinned against Him, and invite Him to live in your heart! Enter the most important relationship of your life! You will never regret it."

By the time the pastor made that call, I was ready. Who could differentiate between tears of repentance and those of joy? Both ran down my cheeks as I responded. I was now a Christian and knew immediately it was the answer to all my questions and the purpose to every life. If it meant the rest of my life would be boring, as I feared, so be it. The truth had set me free and this freedom was not to be used to indulge my sinful nature.

"By the end of my life, Lord, I want to have pleased You more than I've hurt You," I told Him. "For that, I'll have to live a very long time!"

Years passed and I grew in Christ. In 2002 I became a "monthly missionary," driving down every fourth week to Vicente Guerrero, Mexico with Dr. Arnie Gorske, a retired Navy doctor. "Foundation For His

Ministry," which had started as an orphanage in the 1960s, now housed seventy to eighty abused or abandoned children. "The Mission," many called it, had grown to include a Bible School, a day-home for disabled children, paramedic and fire rescue team, and an outreach department. The medical clinic in which we volunteered, attended to children and staff living internally as well as townspeople who lined up outside each morning, mostly poor indigenous farm-workers.

Besides his career as a pediatrician, Dr. Arnie had worked in refugee camps in Viet Nam, with the International Red Cross in Iraq, and gone on forty-five medical mission trips throughout the world. I expected him to fill our drives with tales of personal risk, natural disasters, and miraculous cures.

Instead, on the first trip, he told me, "What the people need most are education and prayer!"

The statement underwhelmed me. Thirty years as a nurse, fourteen years in Intensive Care, I wanted the blood-and-guts stories! Certainly prayer was valuable, but come on! What about the earthquakes and epidemics, all the people your medical teams saved?

"Eighty percent of the diseases that cause most suffering and deaths in developing countries can be prevented," Arnie informed me. "Yet eighty percent of the healthcare that medical teams provide is curative, meaning they hand out medicines after the people are already sick. Also, short-term teams give drugs to people on whom they have sketchy medical histories, won't be able to follow up, not to mention the language and culture barriers! It's a setting in which doctors can do much harm, contrary to their Hippocratic Oath! Education and prevention can save far more lives than drugs, with no harmful side effects!"

Interesting. While this seemed the wrong way to do things considering most of the problems were preventable, at that time his words were just a healthy seed planted in my mind. True understanding of the harm missionaries could inflict on the poor would come later.

Meanwhile, my arrivals at the orphanage began to feel like a homecoming, the month between a waiting period. During a visit in March of 2007, we attended *sala*, the daily worship service for the workers. While everyone was singing praise in Spanish, I heard the voice of God.

"Come to me, here!" He whispered.

Arresting, shocking, yet unmistakable! The call had two dimensions: certainly it was a command, to be obeyed or rejected, but more, it was an invitation.

The beckoning of a Lover, "Come to me, here!"

As with any passionate relationship, the one who is called knows no greater pleasure than to run into the waiting embrace.

So I began to rearrange my life, my thinking, my heart, to spend one year at the orphanage. Letting go of what was behind and straining toward what was ahead, I gave myself six months to transition.

Finally, October had come and like those who had lost their homes, my world as I knew it was ending.

Several times, packing up carton after carton of useless knick-knacks, I considered the up side of an all-consuming fire. The Lord was prying loose my grip on the world and its "stuff." He had a prepared a path that would rock my comfortable five-star world and take "boring" out of my vocabulary.

In fact, had I been able to see the full length of the road ahead, I might have put my knick-knacks back where they belonged.

October 28, 2007

2007

October 30, 2007
Dear Friends,

This is my first letter as a missionary, in partnership with you, and I write with better understanding of the biblical phrase "sacrifice of praise!"

In the movie, *Private Benjamin,* a pampered, somewhat-ditsy woman joined the army. She believed it would be like the photograph the recruiter had shown her – high-rise condominiums overlooking a bay dotted with gleaming white sailboats. Later in the movie, we see her marching through heavy rain at night, exhausted and broken by weeks of barracks, bullies and boot camp.

As she plods in an endless circle, she whines to anyone who might be listening, "This is a huge mistake! This isn't the army I signed up for; I signed up for the one with the condos and the sailboats!"

The movie, of course, ends happily with a stronger, wiser Goldie Hawn walking alone down a path to new life.

Yesterday, when they showed me the trailer I would live in, I, too, felt someone had made a huge mistake. It was the sort of thing we used to see in back yards of New Hampshire, something folks with few teeth and suspenders used as housing for their out-of-luck cousins or aging parents. The shower was broken and the toilet leaked. There was nothing you'd call decor, just lopsided cabinets, worn carpet, and constant dust blowing in through a broken window.

Since I planned to cook my own meals, I had requested "a nice kitchen." (Someone's still laughing at that one!) In an area *maybe* large enough to make Margaritas, sat a tiny sink and two-burner hot plate. The trailer's refrigerator could have held a six-pack and sandwich meat, but not a month's worth of health-food from the States. There was neither a freezer nor an oven.

I did not cry out loud, a mark of some restraint. Still, a strong urge tempted me to run back to Carlsbad and throw myself down on my comfortable bed in my comfortable home and have a tantrum. However, the bed was in storage, my house was leased to strangers, and a friend at the mission had the good sense to pray that I would not obsess about my living quarters. Slowly, I took some deep breaths and turned to the Lord. He reminded me of my commitment to praise Him in all things, a vow made before knowing what those "all things" were.

This is to be a time of praise, not because He gives me the condos and the sailboats, but because He is deserving of all our praise all the time.

Today I opened a devotional book to a random page and found this verse, Romans 8:32:
"He who did not spare His own Son, but gave Him up for us all- how will He not also, along with Him, graciously give us all things?"

Below it was a quote from John Flavel: "Surely if He would not spare His own Son one stroke, one tear, one groan, one sigh, one circumstance of misery, it can never be imagined that ever He should, after this, deny or withhold from His people, for whose sakes all this was suffered, any mercies, any comforts, any privilege, spiritual or temporal, which is good for them."

So please, will you join me in my "sacrifice of praise?" Help me thank Him for these quarters, His gift to me!

United in Him,
Ellie

November 2, 2007
Hello Friends,

Has it been a year yet? Seems like it. I won't lie; it's been very difficult adjusting. There's no doctor in the clinic, and I don't have the heart to tell patients who have waited outside for hours that they can't be seen. So I invite them in and listen as they relate their stories and their symptoms. So often it is their stories that produce their symptoms - poverty, abuse, ignorance, and backbreaking farm labor cause fatigue, headaches, muscle aches, heartburn, and depression.

"They want some magic formula to take away all their problems!" I told a visiting nurse. "A woman comes in because of a headache, but really, what she wants is that someone make her husband stop using drugs and hitting her! I give her Tylenol, instruct her to drink more water, and pray. Still, she sits there, staring down at the capsules in her hand with huge sad eyes, then back at me. Finally, I have to ask her to leave because the other patients are waiting!"

Still, I love these humble people and God called me here. Hadn't He confirmed it when I doubted? More than once, I thought back to the disturbing call I'd received from my mother this summer.

"Ellie, Dad fell and broke his hip! He's going to have surgery tomorrow."

My father was eighty-five years old. He'd already had five-vessel open heart surgery. Any nurse recognized the ominous phrase "fell and broke a hip," often the beginning of a downhill slide for the aged.

"What am I doing, Lord?"

I sank into my couch and cried out loud, like a lost child. It was the middle of my six months preparation time: working, saving, looking ahead – not back! But my father! With that call, all my plans collapsed.

"My parents are old! These are the last years of their lives. I'm their daughter - a nurse, yet! - and instead of moving closer, I'm moving further away! I need to hear from you, Lord! Please, God, tell me what to do!"

The devotional, *My Utmost For His Highest,* lay on the coffee table. I grabbed it and opened to the date – July second. There, at the top of the page, was the most clearly-divine message of my life.

"If anyone comes to Me and does not hate his father and mother, wife and children, brothers and sisters, yes, and his own life also...And whoever does not bear his cross and come after me...So likewise, whoever of you does not forsake all that he has cannot be my disciple."
(Luke 14:26-27, 33)

My tears changed to amazement. God had answered me! *He* would take care of my family! I just had to obey.

That assurance had strengthened me then and several times since. The Lord kept His end of the deal, of course - my father had recuperated from the surgery like a forty-year old and was already walking two miles a day!

God is faithful and gives me gifts whenever I need them. The gifts come in the form of prayer, encouragement, support, children's love, and the best one - a dose of His presence.

November 4, 2007

In *sala*, our morning worship service, a man giving testimony said, "Faith is not just believing God in your mind. Faith must be put into action in order to move your trust from your mind to your heart."

So, talking about being a missionary is faith still in the mind, but each day that I am here, trusting the Lord when life is hard or scary, moves Him into my heart. In countless ways He shows me His faithfulness. Yet He withholds answering every worldly desire so that I may be satisfied more in Him than in His gifts. I have given Him permission to continue even if I whine.

The other night, I spoke to Ofelia and Angel, the parents of a microcephalic girl who died two years ago. With only ten percent of the normal brain matter, she had been unable to talk or sit up. Her spine was bent from severe kyphosis and her eyes wandered in constant motion without ever focusing. Berenice had been one of our regular patients when I used to come down each month with Dr. Gorske.

"Is she able to tell when you're around her?" Arnie had asked once through translation.

"Oh, yes!" Ofelia told us in Spanish. "She smiles when one of her siblings is near and when Angel comes home after being gone all day, she gets very excited and won't stop making noise until he gives her attention!"

Berenice's smile had been angelic; anyone paying attention had to know he or she was in the presence of someone special to God. Her death, at age seven, though expected, was still heartbreaking. Afterwards, Ofelia decided to work with severely-handicapped children to honor her. Angel, the father, was working with teenagers, a request made to him by another daughter just before she died of Leukemia at age seventeen.

There is so much suffering here! Yet people like this couple, who trust God through intense trials, become stronger in faith and models to those watching. My suffering to adjust is baby's breath compared to the hurricane this family's been through.

Still, Angel listened to my story with compassion, not judgment. He smiled when I called myself a *princesa* from the States.

"You came here as a princess but you'll return as a queen!"

My blank look elicited his explanation.

"God has to take things away from us, bring us down low, so that He can raise us up! You came to Mexico as a princess of the world, but you'll return as a queen in His kingdom, and more useful to Him!"

Words like this, when spoken by someone who has suffered great loss, have spiritual power. They created in me a desire to grow, to open myself to whatever circumstances I needed to grow that kind of faith!

November 7, 2007

Wanting to open myself to growth opportunities and walking into a filthy shack to change the pus-laden dressings of a paraplegic man are worlds apart. With the first, you can imagine yourself praying for someone in a simple house or playing with darling children, giving them toys, clothes, or a word from God.

The reality, however, was trying to attend to a patient's needs in the worst hygiene imaginable: dirt floor, no clean spot to lay our supplies and a thousand flies buzzing around my head or landing on the rotted flesh. The smell of Andres' infected wounds was so repulsive it was hard to speak or encourage him. Joy, the nurse with me, didn't seem to notice; she acted as if we were in sterile quarters.

"Oh, these look so much better, Andres!" she said. Turning to me, she told me, "Before, you could see the bone!"

The young man shouted, "Halleluiah!"

We put a new foam pad on his bed and covered him with a relatively clean blanket. He moaned as though he'd just grabbed the chocolate off his pillow and plopped onto a king-size bed at the Ritz.

***

In a moment of clarity during a morning jog, I decided to ask you to pray that God continue His work in me. (I wrote that quickly lest I change my mind and have you pray instead for a comfortable bed, a full-time doctor, or a dozen other selfish desires.) The choice is yours - whether you pray for the old princesa or the distant queen-in-the making.

May God give you what you need each day and may you be content!

I love you all, Ellie

Tales of A Five-Star Missionary

November 10, 2007

Yesterday during lunch, I hosted some children from the "Mefiboseth Ministry," a daycare for the handicapped.

Javier, the oldest of two brothers with Muscular Dystrophy and who calls me *doctora* even though I've told him many times I'm an *enfermera*, (nurse) asked to see my apartment. Little Miguel, who was recuperating fantastically from his cleft palate surgery, opened the door for us and I pushed Javier's wheelchair into my kitchen.

By the way, for those of you who have been concerned about my "trailer," it turned out that the Lord gifted me with a little apartment instead. Perhaps God didn't want to take away my "five stars" too abruptly, or maybe the young man in the office just didn't want to listen to me complain. Anyway, I am much happier!

"Tu casa!" Javier and Miguel yelled over and over, like they had entered a castle.

I stretched out their tour of the tiny apartment as long as possible, then wheeled Javier back outside. The other children from the ministry had seen them enter, though, and began to shout, *"Yo, yo!"* ("Me, me!")

So those who could, wheeled themselves, and the ones who could not, their caregivers or I helped, and soon a circle of wheelchairs crowded my kitchen. The children delighted in a painting of me as a clown and photos of my nieces and nephews. Domitila, a gorgeous little girl with Spina Bifida, pushed herself towards the entry to my bedroom and whispered to the others, *"Es su cama!"* ("That's her bed!")

I'm not quite sure why it was such a big deal for them to learn I had a private life but I felt like a guide in my own anthropological museum.

Mary, the program director and my dear friend, came to collect them.

She scolded them lightly for invading my privacy, but I assured her they were welcome.

"You made their day!" she told me, "but I don't want them to get in the habit. You'll never have a quiet lunch!"

"No, Mary! They made *my* day!"

These special children blessed me in a manner I'd never known and would teach me much about the kingdom of God.

November 11, 2007

Something has changed. All week fog had enclosed the mission each morning and clouds kept everything gray until sunset. Then the skies would clear long enough for the Lord to dazzle us with color just before "the putting away of the sun" or *la puesta del sol* as the Mexicans romantically call it.

Today, however, no cloud dimmed the glory of the day. The sun was already strong at six-thirty, the air as clean as the constant dirt and dust would allow. Running through the orchard, I also felt renewed. Rows and rows of mounded dirt, irrigated with a drip system, sprouted the first green leaves of the strawberry crops. Their gentleness of color made it seem like spring had arrived out of season. Marveling at how many there were, I could easily look ahead to when these fields would be fully grown and laden with red fruit.

I am the same, I thought. The first tiny bud of growth has occurred in me. My concerns are starting to drop away as I drink the Living Water. I am, as always, impatient - wanting to skip ahead to the time of full maturity and fruit, but the winter must come first. If I were as patient as God has been with me, I'd need nothing. He gives us all good things in His time.

November 14 2007

Dr. Luis was visiting for a week from Chicago, a huge, if temporary, relief.

"I'll help you do anything! You don't know how good it feels to have a doctor here!"

He'd studied medicine in Bolivia and Spanish was his first language, but also spoke English with no accent. He was compassionate, tireless, and knowledgeable.

"Teach me anything you think will help me attend to patients when you're not here, please!" I begged him.

He took time during each patient visit to do so. Then a fifty-eight year old man who looked seventy, came in with his wife. His complaint was shortness of breath, but had also had problems with urinary retention off and on for five years. Men are routinely screened for Prostate Cancer in the US with a simple lab test called PSA. Since urinary retention is an early symptom of prostate enlargement, in the States a doctor would have ordered a PSA immediately on a man with that complaint.

However, this man told us firmly, "No, no one's ever drawn any blood.

Dr. Luis did a rectal exam and felt an enlarged hard prostate, an ominous finding.

"Please go have this test done at the lab and bring back the result!" he told the man in Spanish.

When he returned, Luis and I read the lab slip at the same time. Surreptitiously, we gave each other "the look" you never want to see on a healthcare worker's face. The PSA was extremely high, the white mass on his chest x-ray was most likely lung metastases, and the prognosis, terminal.

Luis took the couple in a quiet room and gave them the bad news with great compassion.

"Please, I would like you to come to our church tonight so we can pray for you. Are you Christians?"

The wife said she was but as for her husband, "not really."

"Yes, I'll come," the man asserted.

That evening when the pastor gave an invitation, this same man walked to the front of the church and invited Christ to live in his hurting heart. Just like that, his life was lost and then found in the same day.

Pastor Avitia told me later, "I don't give the invitation every week but tonight the Holy Spirit nudged me."

How great is our God!

November 21, 2007

Miguel, the cutest kid in the world, wore a new pair of gloves to sala, our worship service. They were knit with bold red stripes against black, and he was enamored with them. When anyone patted him on the head or greeted him with an "Hola, Miguel!" the charismatic three-year old would hold up both hands with his fingers fanned to show them off.

The boy's speech was delayed by a cleft palate, but only a few weeks after his second surgery, the few words he did speak were clearer. Still, he was more of an observer and each time he pointed out his new hand apparel, he'd watch his audience for his or her reaction. Although most people gave a "Wow!" or a quick inspection, no one seemed impressed enough to satisfy him. His huge brown eyes would study the person even after he or she walked away.

This child, who in his three years, had watched too many people walk away, suffered a little every time his mittens - and therefore, he - were undervalued.

Until Chabela. Nine year old Chabby, as she was called at the mission, was taken from a dumpster when she was two days old. A policeman found her and DIF, the Mexican Social Service organization, brought her to the orphanage. Severely autistic, she would not let the nursery workers hold her, arching her body backwards until they put her down. Within months of unstoppable love and affection, she changed and wanted to be held all the time.

Now she was nine. She lived with Debby and Murray, Canadian missionaries who continued to transform her through patient and faithful love. Chabby still had severe behavioral problems and didn't interact well with other children. When she did connect with someone, though, staring into their eyes from three inches away or gracing someone with a clumsy smile, it was considered a great gift.

Children in sala often scanned the benches then ran to sit with someone they knew. Miguel chose Murray this morning and climbed into his lap. Chabby, sitting in the next seat, was a little put out and started rocking. Miguel unfazed, leaned over and stuck a gloved hand in her face.

Maybe it was the bright red that caught her attention, but that little glove was now her world. She moved her whole body closer and leaned down so her face was almost touching the yarn. It was as if the hand were a magnet, drawing her. She examined the glove like a slide under a microscope, more intensely than anyone had, even Miguel!

As she studied his prize possession, Miguel studied her, first curious, then playful. He moved the fingers of the glove and turned his hand over, all the time watching her reaction. When she looked up at him and smiled, he went giddy with joy. He giggled and hugged her and she did not reject him. Miguel had received from her the intense response he had not found in anyone else and Chabela interacted on a level unusually intimate for her. These two wounded lambs had reached out and met each other's deepest needs.

All this time the pastor had been preaching on the Lord's Prayer.

"Prayer is a means to submit to God's will," he told us. "We should not just talk to God, but also listen and try to find what He has for us to do today!"

It was a wonderful sermon. Yet, the communion between these two children was more profound. I *had* just listened to God, telling me if I could meet one person's needs as dearly as had Miguel and Chabby, I would have a successful day.

Murray and Chabela

Miguel with His Gloves

November 24, 2007

Miguel and I went to the beach, just the two of us. I was nervous as we drove away from the mission. What if this smiling three-year old got homesick for more familiar faces? The beach was four miles down a lonely road full of rocks and ditches. It would take an eternity to drive it with an inconsolable screaming toddler.

But things started well. He made sure I knew our destination, pointing ahead and saying, *"playa!"* about a thousand times. I assured him it was coming up "pronto!" When we climbed the last small incline and the ocean came into view, his face looked like Christmas had come.

We ran down the hard-packed sand to the water. The tide pools were a disappointment as nothing moved, so we chased seagulls and tossed a few shells back into the ocean. Then we entered the waves. In five minutes little Miguel went from sticking his toe into the cold film of a retreating wave to running into the breakers like a linebacker.

His tiny sweat pants got wet even though I'd rolled up the legs and he looked at me with a mischievous smile every time a wave got him. Soon the waterlogged pants kept slipping down, and in order to run, he had to keep one hand gripping the waist. I debated what a good mother would do and decided his joy was worth the risk of pneumonia. Off came the pants.

Now he entered into the fullness of the adventure, as free as a seagull and silly with joy. I was right there with him, getting soaked by the cold waves and laughing like we were the same age - three. I did have the presence of mind to teach him that the beach and the waves were gifts from God for us to enjoy and we yelled, *"gracias, Dios!"* at the top of our lungs. But mostly we played and ran and laughed out loud.

A moment came as I ran beside this precious child that I wished with all my heart I could keep him from ever returning to a life of poverty. But I knew his mother may return one day and take him to live in a dirt-floor shack with no electricity. That this darling of the mission may grow up to be a migrant worker, laboring for unfair wages, distressed me. Yet, for at least for one warm November day, he was carefree - running, playing, laughing, and being loved; the birthrights of a child.

November 28, 2007

Sometimes I love being a nurse and sometimes I'd like to work anywhere besides the clinic. Today was the latter. A robust baby boy had been seen by a doctor in town and sentenced to three days of intramuscular antibiotic injections. His crime: showing symptoms of a virus cold – cough, congestion, runny nose.

Since my arrival, people had come to us after local doctors had ignored their symptoms of Prostate Cancer, seizures, and chest pain. Yet, for some reason, they unloaded the pharmacy on a common viral cold. It grieved me to know they were creating antibiotic-resistant germs, but it was maddening to give painful injections that weren't even indicated!

The first two doses had been administered by a nurse in town, but, after that, the hospital had run out of that particular antibiotic. So, the mom came to see if we had the medicine and since we did, nurse Ellie, who herself had a cold, got the ugly job of sticking an innocent child's rump! With a pout, I drew up the medicine, knowing I was doing more harm than good.

Luis, who should have been in class, had been following me around. He was eight and had a congenital bowel problem which banned him from the public schools. The Mefiboseth program for disabled children accepted him some months ago, but sometimes, as now, he wandered off. He came from a troubled home; his father, in and out of jail. Yet Luis was gentle and helpful; often we'd see him pushing the wheelchairs of his friends. Also, the boy loved to pray. It was this last trait that saved my day.

He had visited me in my apartment during lunch, then followed me to the clinic. Mary, the program director, later scolded me lightly, saying, "We've warned Luis he is not to leave school without permission! He knows better! Please, if he does it again, send him back!"

His presence was so benign that patients accepted him and I never thought to ask him to leave. He was quiet and interested in everyone's needs.

The mother of the baby wrapped her arms around her young son's body like a vise in preparation for the shot, but I asked her to relax a moment.

"This is my assistant," I told her in Spanish.

The boy smiled shyly at the title, but I was not playing.

"Luis, will you please pray for God to comfort the baby during the injection and to heal him?"

Promptly, with little sense of self, he bowed his head, touched the baby's shoulder and prayed. His petition was simple, but intimate and faith-filled. His manner of prayer reminded us that God was real and listening.

Then, feeling much better myself, I administered the medication into the fat little gluteus. The baby let out an abbreviated whimper and Mom stared at Luis.

"He cried so hard with the other shots!" she told him. "This time was much easier!"

My assistant showed no spiritual pride. He simply looked glad, and his gladness filled the room. Prayer really does change things.

Jose Pushing Feliciano

December 5, 2007

What is Christmas if not for miracles? An unwed homeless virgin had the child of God. This year I will share some things in common with Mary: unwed and about to have a child of God. (The similarities end there.)

Little Miguel, was living with Dirk and Mary, an exceptional couple who had moved from the Netherlands to Canada to Mexico. These are people I'd dare anyone not to like; each of them full of love, joy, and kindness. God used them to snare me because He knew I couldn't refuse them anything.

"Ellie, I need to talk with you, ask a favor," Mary said with her slight Dutch accent. Her expression was concerned and direct. I braced myself.

"Can you watch Miguel while we're gone?"

Watch him? Sure, that's what I like to do with kids - watch them, play with them, and then return them to whomever.

"You mean live with him?"

Yes, that was what she meant.

"I know how you've bonded and he would get more one-on-one attention with you than if he stays with Bonnie, since she already has two babies."

She gave me time to think. During *sala* that morning, I watched Miguel. Part of me leaped at the privilege of spending more time with this precious boy. Another part imagined him as a tiny monster, waiting for the chance to abuse his new and inexperienced *tía* (aunt.)

Some people have a deep fear that if they convert to Christianity, God will call them to Africa or some faraway jungle. This never concerned me since I loved to travel and Africa, in fact, was one of my favorite journeys. Still, plenty of missionaries *did* get called to dangerous lands. Jim Elliott and his friends were speared to death by the very people they came to save.

God was calling me to a place far scarier: a fifty-four year old bachelorette, whose hobbies included silent prayer, reading, writing, and jogging – all things done alone and in silence – to live twenty-four hours a day with a mischievous toddler.

Dirk came in as reinforcement.

"You know, this little guy is so afraid of being alone! This morning when he got up, I had gone to pick up some of the other children and Mary was in the shower. So, for a few minutes he couldn't find us. Mary said when she came out of the shower, his little face showed panic!"

"Ok, ok; I'll do it!" I said.

"You're an answer to our prayers," he told me.

"Pretty feeble answer," I said, "but it does prove, *'His ways are not our ways!'*"

The next few nights I woke up at odd hours with anxiety due mostly to selfishness. *I won't be able to go jogging! I won't be able to write! I'll have to cook him the disgusting things that kids like, whatever that is!* But this nightly distress was diminishing and I was starting to believe that God could provide mothering skills to someone who didn't even know what a three-year old ate.

So one week from tomorrow, I'll become a mom. If I haven't yet asked for specific prayer, now I definitely am! Mothers, you know the prayers I should be asking for, so pray them, please! I look ahead with great anticipation and the desire to give this wounded angel love and a special Christmas.

I'm sure it will be better than getting speared through by natives.

Miguel and Domitila

December 9, 2007

In the bog of mud between three shacks, we set a metal tub and baptized six people with pails of water. The boys with Muscular Dystrophy had to be lifted in their chairs and then set in the tub. Dirk helped David, who was performing the baptisms, strip twelve-year old Javier to the waist. The sight of his skeletal body nearly suffocated us with grief.

Yet his faith was huge and he yelled to be first, *"Yo primero!"* In the tub, he started to shiver and scream, *"Frío! Frío!"* (cold!)

Dave stopped everything and asked him, "Javier, do you want to be baptized?"

The kid and the kidding disappeared. In a mature and confidant voice, he answered, *"Sí!"*

He shrieked again as the water poured over him but it blended with our shouts of joy. His brother, little Feliciano, was so sweet and frail that the thought of dumping cold water on him seemed abusive. However, he, too, took it seriously, afraid of the cold shower but nodding to David to continue. Their sister, Mary, Uncle Ascensión, and Aunts Carmen and Victoria, followed.

We celebrated with pizza and prayer. On the way home, Dirk, Mary and I were discussing the chain of ministers God used to bring about this glorious day.

"First Elia, (a local missionary) discovered Javier and Feliciano living on the floor of a shack!" Mary said.

"Then my friends, Gloria and Dolores, told Elia to bring the boys to the mission to be seen by Dr. Arnie," I added.

Mary went on.

"Arnie referred them to Dirk and he made both boys special wheelchairs. Then we brought them into the Mefiboseth program."

Dirk continued, "David and Carrie Irving started a Bible study in the grandma's home, which led to the baptisms!"

Obviously, God had planned it before the creation of the world.

December 11 2007

Last night I had to stay in the clinic until seven p.m. because a doctor was seeing patients. No one asked me; it was just assumed I would stay. Usually the clinic closed at five, I cooked dinner and ate. So hunger was a handy excuse, but the truth was I was just irritated at having to work two hours overtime without pay and without being asked.

The patients were old men from a home for the elderly. And the fact that the *doctora* was also serving for free did not keep me from wishing she would hurry up. The doctor had her own nurse with her, who was also her fiancé. My sole responsibility was to be there while they worked and to lock up when they left.

After tiring of playing on the Internet, I went out and greeted a couple of the men waiting to be seen. They were friendly Christians and eager to experiment with the little English they knew.

"How do you call thees een Eenglish?" one lean gentle-eyed man asked.

He was miming using a broom.

"Sweep" I answered.

He could not pronounce the word near correctly but told me, "I want swoob."

I got him a broom from the closet and he began to "swoob" the waiting room, moving chairs, picking up trash - an excellent job. Without pausing in his self-assigned task, he asked in Spanish, "Are you Christian?"

"Yes, sure," I answered.

"Then you understand," he said with smiling eyes. "I like to sweep for Jesus. I don't sweep for you; I sweep for Jesus. You understand?"

Yes, suddenly I did. I had been praying for the grace to do everything in my life for Jesus, especially with patients, but clearly, the evening more clearly showed love for self.

When the last patient had been treated, we all went home, me with the feeling that God had just spoken through a leathery old man with a broom.

And in case I hadn't gotten it, a visiting pastor preached the same message the next morning. He read the part of Scripture where Mary anointed Jesus with the bottle of expensive perfume. Then he asked us which disciple we thought was the best. People guessed Peter, John, others.

"Is it possible that the best disciple was a woman?" he suggested.

Then he went on to tell the three times this Mary was in the Bible.

"First, at a party in her home, when her sister is rushing about, we find her sitting at the feet of Jesus. After Lazarus dies, Martha gets pretty confrontational with Jesus, but Mary is more humble, asking submissively, *"Where were you, Lord?"* Finally, we find her washing Jesus' feet with her hair and anointing his body with perfume. So every time we see her, she is at the feet of Jesus."

He reminded us that people didn't often bathe in those days so this perfume would have remained on Jesus for a long time.

"When he was being questioned by the high priests and denied by Peter, the scent of the perfume would have been with Him. When He was being mocked and whipped, He would be able to smell the scent. And finally on the cross, suffering and dying, the sweet fragrance would have been with Him."

"How many people in the Bible minister to Jesus? Everyone wants something *from* Jesus; Mary ministered *to* Him. She sat at His feet, she poured herself out for Him, she ministered to Him."

Then this pastor urged us, "Today, minister to Jesus!"

I thought of Mother Teresa, who spoke of seeing Jesus in "His distressing disguise as the poor." My old man with the broom and the happy eyes, he had ministered to Jesus.

Dear Lord, I prayed, *let me see you today, every day, in each person, in each task!*

If only I had worked those two hours last night for Jesus, and not blown the chance to dab my sweet Savior with perfume!

December 16 2007

Miguel's favorite word was *caballo* which meant "horse" in Spanish. He used it as a substitute for any word he didn't know, as a persuasion tactic because he knew he was adorable and funny when he said it, or as an expression of delight. So when two stray, but real, horses showed up Friday morning nibbling the grass in front of our apartment, I took it as a sign that everything was indeed going to be caballo!

So it started. Dirk and Mary left mid-afternoon and Miguel hardly seemed to notice. We had dinner with two extra places set for Zebra and brand new Blancoso, a white Christmas bear sent to him by a woman in my church. I tied the bear's hands together with a rubber band so he could pray with us. It was Norman Rockwell gone Hispanic.

As I read his bedtime story he cuddled and joked, exploding into gales of laughter then listening to the Christmas tale with a child's wonder. Bedtime was just as Dirk had told me.

"He will feel for the warmth of your neck and put his face against it. Then he turns over and is fast asleep."

He did this while hugging my neck and when he turned his little back to me, he seemed so tiny and vulnerable; I lay there for several minutes just loving him and praying for him. Then I went out of his room.

The morning started as great. He slept through the night and wandered into my room at six. He gave me so many hugs and kisses on my cheek, I thought things were caballo. We ate buckwheat pancakes and sliced apples; then it was time to get ready for a clown event.

"Make him your assistant!" Dirk had suggested when I told him about the commitment. "He will love it!"

Claudia, in the sewing room, had sewed him a clown suit, white with colored dinosaurs, red fringe on the wrists and ankles. He never lost interest during the hour it took me to apply my makeup and even helped me brush the powder off my face. Then I brought his suit out, shaking the fringe.

"No!" he said, pointing to the suit and shaking his head. He smiled but his eyes were serious.

"Come on!"

He liked this English phrase and usually mimicked me when I said it. He smiled but answered with a firm, "No!"

"Tú y yo!" I encouraged him, pointing to him then myself, *"Payasos!"* (Clowns.)

A big smile. A finger straight at me.

"Tú, sí; yo, no."

That was that. I quickly gave him some blue eyebrows, a couple of green glitter dots on his cheekbones, red lips, and threw the custom-made costume in the car in case he changed his mind.

The Christmas outreach was in a nearby village, Zapata. As soon as we stepped from the car, one hundred and twenty children mobbed the clown. They surrounded me, untied the big bow around my waist and tried to pull me around by the sashes, and grabbed the "Jesus Loves You" stickers out of my hand. The local missionary-*pastora* had a great smile and the greenest eyes but not a hint of control over the kids.

"I'm just going to do a few gospel magic tricks and help hand out the backpacks. Forget about the balloons!" I told her.

Miguel did not get the one-on-one attention he needed. By the time we got home, drained and tired, he refused to go in the house.

"Mi, allá," he said. ("Me, there,") pointing to Bonnie's.

Bonnie was taking care of two baby girls while Betty and Phil were gone for two months. Miguel had lived there with them, but moved to Dirk and Mary's when "Mama Betty and Papa Phil" left – quite an adjustment for any toddler, but traumatic for a boy abandoned by his real dad and separated from his mom. We had thought he'd be better off alone with me than sharing attention with the girls. However, we had not considered his need for stability. He showed us our mistake.

Bonnie welcomed him in to play with his buddies, Lucy and Valeria, while I got out of my foolish costume. When I went to bring him home for supper he cried. When we got inside our apartment, he went ballistic. He yelled and sobbed. He kicked the door. When I tried to hug him, he threw a fist and followed it with a kick. I left him alone after that and started dinner.

But he was inconsolable, helplessness coming in heavy gasping sobs. Anyone who has cried like that could recognize the sound of a broken heart. All the pain and loss of the world were in the room with us, breaking my heart, too! He was no longer young. I spoke to him with respect and acknowledgement.

"Miguel, I understand!"

His forlorn eyes met mine from across the kitchen. I determined to overcome his fear with love.

"I know that you miss Papa Cate and Mama Mary!"

He grew alert, cried louder. He shook his head and screamed, "No!"

Three-years old and he was already burying sadness with anger.

"I know it's hard – first Betty and Phil, now Dirk and Mary!"

I did not mention his parents.

"But they're coming back! They didn't want to leave you! They love you! They just have to visit their families, and then they'll come back to be with Miguel, you!"

The reassurance must have sunk in because we had a nice dinner and story. He lost it again when he went to bed, though, and instead of hugging, he cried himself to sleep. So did I.

The morning seemed better until we went outside. He ran over to Bonnie's again, and together, we made the decision to honor his desire.

So, like that, my motherhood was over. It was devastating to be rejected by this child I loved. I cried when I went through the apartment, throwing clothes and toys into a laundry basket to officially move him.

However, the story is Miguel's, not mine. I am an adult and a missionary. He is an abandoned child, whom I came to serve. If I can serve him better by giving him up, I will delight in watching him play with his two *hermanas.* If he wants me for a tía and not a mamá, then so be it. God is in control, of his life and mine.

And as long as that's true, "Caballo!"

Miguel Praying

Caballo!

December 26, 2007

I expected to have a heartwarming Christmas story from the orphanage, an encounter of love and grace equal to the miracle of the Incarnation. And I do, sort of.

The Advent season is not marred here with the madness of holiday shopping and office parties. Two thousand years after Christ brought holiness to earth, the Spirit still enchants those poor enough to notice.

We noticed when we went caroling through slums and migrant camps. We noticed when filthy children smiled shyly and received their gifts. We noticed when we walked the mission grounds in silence on a crisp starry night.

My spirit rejoiced as I watched Miguel open his first Bible, a toddler's version and my present to him. His eyes gleaming, and with all the time in the world, he studied each page twice before handing it back so I'd read to him. His first gift so enthralled him that even the wrapping paper seemed a treasure. He folded it neatly and saved it. Bonnie and I oohed and aahed.

That was two days before Christmas. After that the trail of grace vanished. On the twenty-fourth, having promised a Christmas eve dinner for some people, I drove to *Alianza*, the town's largest market.

Mushrooms, tomatoes, and cucumbers.

Going over my list in my mind, I never noticed the puddle. So when I fell, it surprised me and I did nothing to cushion the landing. Various body parts reported to my brain - right knee, shoulder, both palms. I lay prone a few minutes, contemplating the disgustingly filthy floor. Several people spoke, scuffled, pushed carts around me. I expected a crowd to rush over and help me, to inquire about my injuries.

But no one came.

A gush of self-pity and loneliness hit hard. Rising slowly, I hobbled through the vegetable aisle, ignoring the crowd now and alienating myself further through my thoughts.

I'm alone, far from family or friends. A missionary, and the people I came to serve don't even care about me. Well, this is just great!

I wanted to cry but refused to embarrass myself further. A couple of Tylenols, a hot shower, and a nap helped.

Then came Christmas Eve. We ate and watched Miguel open many presents. Gone were the wonder and slow savoring of his gifts. Bonnie and I looked at each other, shocked at how quickly he had learned greed. Christmas Day he opened still more, and still more he showed lust and a reluctance to share.

Grace peeked through in short bursts as we delivered food and clothes to families we knew outside the mission, but I went to bed as drained and spent as if I'd gone to the malls and office parties.

Today, however, when I rose in the early dawn and sat quietly with the Lord, He reminded me it was not Miguel, nor even the poor, I came to serve. It was Jesus Christ Who called me, Who sustained me, and Who would restore my soul. That re-knowing changed my view of the past few days. I thought again of when I fell, and took comfort in the knowledge that I had not been alone or unnoticed. Miguel's precious face came and reminded me that God was only beginning to teach and transform him.

When I walked out to face the day, the whole San Quintin Valley shone with new hope. A day late, I recognized that, indeed, the Spirit of Christ had been born again into the world.

"And if you spend yourselves in behalf of the hungry and satisfy the needs of the oppressed, then your light will rise in the darkness and your night will become like noonday. The Lord will guide you always. He will satisfy your needs in a sun-scorched land and will strengthen your frame. You will be like a well-watered garden, like a spring whose waters never fail." (Isaiah 58:10-11)

Spoiled Miguel at Christmas

Christmas visit to Domitila's (center)

2008

January 1, 2008

A preacher urged us to look back over our year. He brought us to that part of the Bible when Moses asked God to show him His glory. The Lord granted him his request, saying He would cause all His "goodness" to pass in front of him but that he could not see His face, *"for no one can see my face and live."* The Lord set up the arrangements, telling Moses, *"There is a place near me where you may stand on a rock. When my glory passes by, I will put you in a cleft in the rock and cover you with my hand until I have passed by. Then I will remove my hand and you will see my back; but my face must not be seen."*

The preacher told us, "Jesus Christ is that cleft in the rock. He is our safe place and the place where we can see God's glory. We can look back over our year and see where God has passed by, but we cannot see into the future."

So I reflected and saw evidence that God had indeed guided me, protected and covered me, used, instructed, disciplined and blessed me. But I could no more see what this year had in store for me than anyone else. I have had just as many days here as at home that felt frustrating and confusing. Blessings appeared as glimpses of glory, but they were fleeting and based on circumstances.

Only when I sat in silence before Him, in the cleft of my Rock, gazing upon His glory, only then did I know I was where I was supposed to be, doing what I was meant to do. Then I could go out knowing what was important - the Alpha and the Omega has just passed by and the future was in His perfect loving hands. May I carry a reflection of that glory into my world!

January 17, 2008

Sometimes, despite all the poverty and the problems, this place just blesses me from morning to night. Monday was such a day, and since some of my messages have included complaints about the clinic, let it be said I had a great day being "Nurse Ellie."

We have a new baby. Her name is Yazmín and she is as delicate and feminine as God ever created. Her parents told the staff at the local hospital they didn't want her – yes, you read correctly, they did not want this perfect child. So we got her on her fourth day of life and now she is thirteen days old. She lives with Betty and Phil, a Canadian couple who care for all the newborns and sick babies and who will live in a Bill Gates-size mansion in heaven. I found some flimsy excuse to visit her and started my day marveling at this precious doll and how God swept her out of rejection and made her the darling of the mission.

Next I went to visit Alfredo, a young man terminally-ill from colon cancer. Previously, I had given the family long-acting Morphine pills which, like so many other meds, miraculously appeared at the clinic when I needed them. Along with the medicine I brought some personal supplies and taught the family how to care for him. A few of us gathered around his bed on that day and prayed so hard, I thought for sure he would stand up healed. It didn't happen, but he did open his eyes before we left and with a beatific smile, told us "My pain is gone!"

Today I returned, and found the mother seated in a chair in the driveway, a crowd gathered around her. After nine years as a hospice nurse, it was obvious that the time of crisis was past. Alfredo was gone.

I left the supplies and the extra Morphine tablets in the car. His mother and I held each other for a long time, sharing tears, pain, disappointment, and support.

"Yo había esperado," I told her, meaning "I had hoped..." The unfinished thought was "that God was going to heal him." Yet, the words reminded me of the two disciples on the road to Emmaus. They too, *"had hoped"* for something that seemed not to have come about. They had hoped that Jesus was the one who would redeem Israel. Ultimately, their hope was not disappointed.

"My son is with the Lord!" she told me, and I knew our hope had not been disappointed, either. God had indeed healed her believing son and he would live forever.

I left with a heavy heart mixed with a strange kind of pleasure.

Later, when I was about to cook my dinner, a group of young girls knocked on my door shouting, "The burro bit Rosa!"

How could I not love this place? The medium-sized burro was tied to a stake in the soccer field. The most active I'd seen him was when he was chewing grass. So how these girls had provoked him they didn't reveal, but from their chorus of excited Spanish, I learned that the lazy old burro bit Rocio's finger and wouldn't let go until she pushed him hard *"por cinco minutos!"*

The skin was only broken in a spot as big as a pinhead but the finger was bruised and slightly swollen. So we made a big deal of tramping over, opening the clinic, and with the audience of her friends, I washed and dressed the finger. Then we prayed for her and the burro.

My evening ended with a visit to Dirk and Mary's, now the home of Javier and Feliciano. After a discussion with the boys' grandmother who cares for them, we all agreed the boys would have the best chance for survival through the winter in the warmth and care of the mission.

Mary and Dirk, who volunteered to take the boys into their home, will be on the same street in heaven as Betty and Phil. I hope they'll let me visit whenever I want like I do now.

It was pure joy to watch Javier in his new bathrobe, reclined on the couch, his head on a throw pillow, laughing like he had never enjoyed such luxury. Because, of course, he never had. Feliciano, the younger and weaker, didn't have enough strength to lift his hands all the way, but he brought them up as high as his deteriorating muscles would allow, then got my attention by yelling, "Lollie!" which is how he said my name. I high-fived him then gave him a long hug. Mary played Disney's *Fantasia* on DVD but they were more interested in every photo and knick-knack in their new luxurious home, (a simple two-bedroom apartment.)

Dirk, Mary, and I shared the pleasure of their pleasure and I went to bed praising God for the riches of my day.

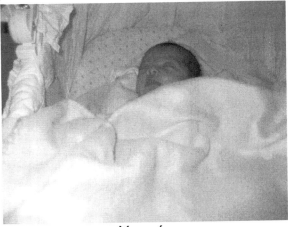

Yazmín

Tales of A Five-Star Missionary

Javier and Feliciano

Tales of A Five-Star Missionary

January 27, 2008

God made me a clown. It's a strange gift – had I been consulted I might have asked for something like pastor or teacher – but I enjoy making people laugh and acting like a fool. The Lord equips.

My clown's name is Luci, and she was thrilled to meet a new clown friend, Verita. We were both trained by the same wonderful couple, Frank and Carol Halowell, who started the Horizon Clown Ministry in San Diego eighteen years ago. Carol put us in touch with each other because she knew we both clowned "somewhere in Baja." By the depth of God's coincidences, the "somewhere in Baja" turned out to be the same place, the mission.

Vera was just finishing a month's visit when we met. She came to my apartment for dinner and we watched a DVD on clown magic.

"You show me some balloon figures and I'll teach you some games!" she suggested.

When the evening ended, the table and floor were covered in balloon animals, torn napkins, a portion of salt and the shaker, glitter, magic-ribbon streamers, a Walt-Disney-meets-Hurricane-Katrina look. We both sat back in our chairs, fed and satisfied.

Yesterday the mission church held an all-day event for boys on a nearby ranch. They had food, games, singing, fun with a Gospel message, and of course, clowns. She wore a lemon yellow wig, and Luci, her usual pink curls, and we drove along a dirt road into the foothills.

"Say hi to the cowboys, Luci!" she shouted.

Lost in our conversation, I hadn't noticed the men on horseback trying to catch our attention. We smiled and waved to our admirers.

The ranch house was brick and settled in a valley. About seventy-five boys from five to fifteen enjoyed the program, designed to feed them in every way.

Verita introduced herself, saying, "I have come from a distant planet and I'm fifteen-thousand years old! My friend, Luci, has come from even further away! She traveled five years to get here today because she heard there were people who did not know about the great love of Jesus Christ!"

Everything went wrong. We ran out of prize-candy early on. The balloons I bought for a "stuff-the-T-shirt" contest were too small and the kids couldn't blow them up. Verita ad-libbed while I grabbed four teenagers. In a manic state, two of us pumped balloons hard and fast and three others tied them until we had fifty and could try the game again.

During the chicken dance, the stocking cap under my wig lost its elasticity. With my real hair loose, the wig kept rising and trying to fall off. I made it through the song with wild gestures, jerking it back in place while I spun, jumped, and glided. My square-dance slip ripped. A pink lock of my wig got stuck in one of my fake eyelashes, exerting a gentle but annoying tug. Then the glue failed on the green-glitter heart on my nose. It slipped off, perhaps to be discovered someday by a confused rancher.

All this happened so God could make it perfect. Verita and I played off each other like sisters. The boys were all smiles and energy, the good news of the Gospel reached their ears, and by grace, their hearts.

Henri Nouwen said, "The wonderful thing about clowns is that they make people unafraid to fail. Clowns live by their mistakes. They act them out in public so others can identify and laugh and go on."

It's the bloopers we'll remember from our wonderful day yesterday, the bloopers that made us human and made us need one another.

Verita and I shared as we drove home.

She confessed to me, "Everytime I get ready to clown, as I'm putting on my makeup, I think, 'Why do I do this? I'm not very good and what's the point?"

I told her, "I do the same thing! I wonder if it does any good at all and if I should spend an hour putting on makeup just to act like a fool!"

But in our hearts we knew it was worth it. God made us *payasas*- that's Spanish for clowns – and we all need to be whom God made us to be. We blunder and bloop and continue, whether saints or sinners or clowns.

Wig Falling Off!

February 10, 2008

Cinderella, Sleeping Beauty, the Princess – the fantasies that little girls love to dream about. Fairy tales always seem to begin with or wander through a time of tragedy. Cinderella lived in poverty and was treated as a slave by her wicked stepmother and sisters, Sleeping Beauty, deceived then poisoned, Rapunzel was imprisoned and lonely.

So, too, the mission abounded with tragic beginnings. Too many Cinderellas to count, abused and treated as slaves, dozens of innocent beauties deceived and poisoned by incest, addictions, abandonment. And of course, each of these would-be princesses suffered from a prison of loneliness when she first arrived.

But yesterday we skipped ahead to the fairy tale ending; we made a day where broken girls on the mend could taste and see that perhaps it was possible to live happily ever after. *"La Fiesta Del Te"* was an annual event, a High Tea for girls and their adult or teenage female escorts. Claudia and Domitila, who ran the Sewing Room, worked miracles for the event. They took donated dresses, shoes and fabric and transformed each girl into a princess. Given the number of those attending (over one hundred) and the randomness of what was donated, it was amazing to see over and over how the perfect dress or gown appeared that we hadn't noticed before, or something grabbed from a pile was the perfect fit, the right shoes, a shawl that matched, or something looked so-so until Claudia transformed it with a few miraculous alterations.

"We'd like you to host the event," some teenagers told me. They were part of the planning committee. "You can do whatever you want, just make it fun!"

Again, I acknowledged that while this was not pastor or teacher, it was what God gave me a love to do. My goal was to help the girls travel to that special place where fun and dreams lifted and thrilled. Claudia outfitted me in a Jessica McClintock white-lace gown and I added a long, straight fuchsia wig. Sort of a ladylike Cher.

Some friends were visiting, Kathy, Linda, and Ida, all ready to help. So we spent the morning curling hair for the special-needs girls. Perhaps Mary and I were prejudiced, but we always said that every one of "our" girls was gorgeous inside and out. Domitila was paraplegic, always in a wheel chair. On her worst day she was merely pretty, but with her shiny black mane in loose curls, she was stunning! We caught her staring at her own reflection in a handheld mirror, and we prayed her dreams come true!

Kenya, obese and hyperactive, was not a likely candidate for the red carpet. But when Kathy took the time to curl her hair then help her into a white off-the-shoulder dress with delicate pink polka-dots, she was transformed.

Then there was Celeste. This petite five-year old was a product of rape, and deaf; maybe she chose not to hear the struggle of her conception. But she was also gorgeous and an adorable concoction of sweet femininity and tough tomboy. With her huge pouty lips colored slightly and waist-long tresses in ringlets, she was as beautiful as an angel.

Tales of A Five-Star Missionary

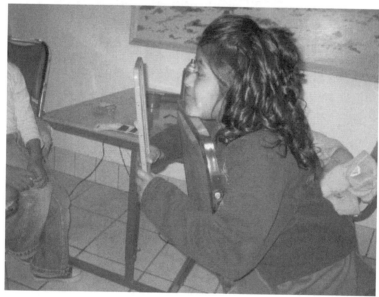

The festivities were insignificant: games and songs, tea and all kinds of baked goodies. What mattered was that they saw themselves and their friends dressed up; their faces glowed with pleasure and excitement.

I opened with a prayer and told them, "God is here and He wants to tell you all how beautiful you are! But He is looking on the inside, not on your dresses. He loves what He sees and says to tell you He made you beautiful inside and out!"

We held a contest to see which of the youngest girls could smile the biggest and one by one, I picked them up and stood them on a chair so all could see this little *princesita*. As she smiled I measured from one corner to the other and then declared the winner.

The middle age group, five to nine, took turns hugging Bethany, a teenager who had helped run the event. This turned out to be my favorite task of the day as I got to help Domitila in her wheel chair, and Zaida and Lupita with walkers get through the long line, as much princesses as anyone standing on her own. Maybe it was cheating, but I prayed for Domi to win and sure enough, Bethany chose her. I pushed her front and center to receive her prize, just as she will do one day in Heaven.

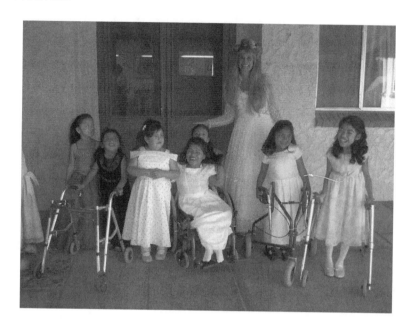

Their Prince had come. They were no longer in rags. His perfect love destroyed the power of evil stepmothers, abuse, abandonment, and neglect. He had conquered the poison of rape and incest, washing away blemishes until all appeared snow-white before Him. By the power of His love and grace, we gave these darlings a glimpse of elegance, true love, and dreams. One day He will come on a white horse; today we must work and pray, that each princess's dreams come true in Him!

February 20, 2008

Through children with special needs I am discovering a unique kind of love, and it hurts. Because in order to love these kids you must enter into their woundedness. There you find a wonderful dance of vulnerability and healing.

Some days I forget that Domi and Alexis are paraplegic, Celeste deaf and neglected, Feliciano and Javier terminally ill. Some days we share so much joy and love that hope rushes in with all kinds of promises.

On other days, poverty and disease poke my heart like bad seeds that refuse to be ignored. This story comes with a documentary-type warning:

"The following contains graphic information which may cause revulsion or heartache. You can skip ahead to a lighter chapter. Or you can enter in to a world that is poor, hurting, and real, a world that needs you to understand and care."

His name was Esteban. We got word of him through other Christians who had built his mother a new home.

"He can't sit up or talk. He's emaciated, filthy, and alone most of the day."

Perhaps this well-intentioned worker had never seen poverty before, or maybe she just misjudged. When we investigated, we found a six-year old boy, severely handicapped by Cerebral Palsy, being loved and cared for to the best of his single mother's abilities. Yes, he was frail and dangerously thin - only fourteen pounds - but disease and intense poverty were the culprits, not the desperate mom.

God went to work immediately to provide the family with miracles.

"Someone donated a special carriage when we were home at Christmas," Dirk had said.

This strange stroller came with padding to support his torso and hold his head upright, special wheels that could manage the rough terrain, and the ability to tilt at an upright angle to prevent him from choking.

"I never imagined what use such a stroller would have for the ministry," Dirk admitted, "but when I put Esteban in the chair, everything fit perfectly to his little body. I did not have to make a single adjustment!"

Eduardo was Esteban's twin and, as if to show us what the world would be like had it not fallen, he shone with health and energy. One could not help comparing the smiling vigorous boy who ran among us to the pointy-featured motionless child struggling on his own phlegm.

Ofelia, part of our visiting team, had cared for Berenice, her special needs child for seven years. She spoke to the mother in a way no one else could, understanding the fierce battles and priceless victories involved in such a life.

As for me, I held Esteban in my arms, rocking him and cooing, and finding that without a word or a sound, this vulnerable being carried me into God's presence. It was a place not unlike prayer, more pure than anything spoken. I longed to be for him whatever he needed, to connect with him so he could know he was loved, and to protect him from all that threatened him. If he received any comfort, I don't know, but he certainly gave me a peace I deeply needed. Holding him told me that, in God's embrace, we were all somehow safe, in spite of the world and its dangers.

He died a week later. Ofelia and I drove to the home to pick up the mother and son and take them to physical therapy. One of the kids let us in. Modesta looked at me in a way that told me everything.

"Hermana, I tried to reach you!" she said. "I sent someone to find you on Sunday, but she forgot your name so she couldn't ask anyone where you lived!"

Her special child had been ripped from her life, yet her concern was that I'd made an unnecessary visit. The gigantic humility of the poor.

He had died peacefully, succumbing to pneumonia, and his memorial service was at three o'clock, forty minutes from now, a fact not lost on us concerning the grace of God. We rushed back to the mission, picked up Dirk and Victor Manuel, his assistant, and dropped off Ofelia, who could not bear another funeral almost two years to the day of burying her own daughter.

The body was in a cold bare room next to the house, lit only by candles. Esteban wore a knit cap and green blanket inside a small wooden casket, covered in white-brocade cloth. Several siblings and cousins ran around, sometimes silent and watching, sometimes playing like an ordinary day. We adults circled the table which held the casket and sang. We lifted up the Bible's promise that there will be, *"no lagrimas nor tristeza,"* no tears or sadness in heaven. Our songs of praise held power and reminded us the battle lost was in a war already won.

Then we loaded the lightweight coffin into a borrowed SUV. That vehicle and mine were the only ones in the funeral procession. As we drove through the rows of graves I wondered if this were a pediatric cemetery - so many of the markers indicated only a few years of life. Dirk commented on the same thing until we saw more adult graves and realized it was just a statistical result of poverty.

"Babies die here," Dirk noted.

The grave had been dug. At most funerals in the States, the casket is lowered by some type of elevator device and the grave filled in later after the friends and relatives leave. Here, the little white box was lowered by hand into the pit on mismatched ropes. Then the boy's father, who had abandoned the family after the tragic birth, shoveled dirt and small rocks into the six-foot hole. The sound of the rocks hitting the lid of the casket prevented illusions. I watched Modesta's face as she bore this unfathomable grief. She was alone in a place no one could reach, the cold, unreal world of a mother burying her son. Mary could have understood, but the mother of Jesus wasn't here. Just a stoic woman staring without sight and an ex-husband laboring to fill the grave of a child he had deserted.

Suddenly I saw the world in which I lived in stark truth. I saw a land of poverty, injustices and oppression, stripped of distance or false hope or tea parties. Strangely, I did not turn away. For this was the world I had come to love. Modesta and her dead son were my heroes.

When I told her, "Ofelia and I want to come back in a few weeks and take you out to lunch," she answered,

"Hermana, mi casa es tuya." My house is yours.

It's true. We had touched hearts and therefore shared a home.

Maybe how much we love depends on how much we are willing to be wounded. And when we are wounded by the same things that wound the heart of God, it is called prayer.

So when I returned home from this day which should have been depressing, I felt blessed. Exhausted and sad, yet blessed.

"How can you explain it?" Dirk asked, for he felt the same as I. "Who would understand how we could feel so blessed from attending a boy's funeral?"

"It is the strange logic of Jesus," I answered. *"He who loses his life for Jesus' sake will find it."*

And the place where often we find it is among the poor.

Tales of A Five-Star Missionary

March 1, 2008

More and more I feel the desire to pray. To rise in the dark and begin my day in the awareness of His great love. To snatch ten minutes after lunch alone with Him. To invite Him into my encounters with the poor so they might become rich. Still, it is never enough.

I recite words from Psalm 63 frequently, *"O God, you are my God, earnestly I seek you; my soul thirsts for you, my body longs for you."*

Yesterday He stirred in me a desire to come apart. *La Cueva del Pirata* seemed just the place for a retreat, a rustic hotel far out a dirt road beside the ocean. The structure is stone and looks half-built because it is, the second floor nothing but frames and wishes.

Victor, the waiter who checked me in, seemed too young and clean-cut to have found Christ in prison, but indeed, he told me this when I mentioned my purpose for coming. Soon we were friends and he loaded one of my Jason Upton CDs into the sound system. The restaurant was empty but for the cook and us two. I chose a table by the window and watched long lazy waves wrap themselves around the bay. My favorite worship music filled the room, and with all the time in the world, I sipped scrumptious coffee and nibbled on papaya, honey, and oatmeal, a halfhearted attempt at fasting.

The room was thirty-four US dollars and came with "hot and cold water." Comfortable, with an ocean view, I entered just long enough to drop off my things then headed out. Easy trails led through hills in full spring blossom.

As I walked I prayed for everyone and everything I could think of, but especially for Enrique, Lucero, and me. Enrique is a story for another day. Lucero is a sweet twelve-month old girl who lives at the mission. She has a blood dyscrasia doctors have not been able to diagnose.

And I, of course, am a woman who needs constant prayer to maintain my lifeline to Christ.

I chose brilliant orange poppies to symbolize my prayers for Enrique, tall yellow wildflowers as those for myself, and the tiny white blossoms close to the earth were for little Lucero. At times I prayed with words, but mostly I just drank in God's refreshing Spirit. The flowers seemed so personal, His attention to my small concerns. Whenever I raised my head, though, and took in the grand views of the Pacific, worship for the infinite God burst out of my mouth like the crashing waves.

Pastor Avitia, the mission's pastor, recently encouraged us to spend time alone with God.

"If everyone does this," he assured us, "the church will be strong and God will transform the San Quintin Valley through His people!"

In Haggai, God tells the people to *"Go up into the mountains and bring down timber and build the house, so that I may take pleasure in it and be honored."*

That's what I was doing as I walked and prayed and worshipped; gathering timber to bring back down.

I even prayed this, "Please Lord, give me strong and precious wood, to use in the next days, so You may take pleasure in my part of the temple and be honored."

March 10, 2008

The inadequacy I feel in ministry no longer bothers me. I trust God to work beyond my efforts or awareness. The key is to be "prayed up," and present in a humble and expectant manner, seeking the Lord's response to someone's needs. Elizabeth showed me just how important that presence can be.

She'd been coming in the clinic with her father, a diabetic. Nurse Joy was faithfully treating a chronic ulcer on his foot and with her perseverance and prayer, it had begun to heal.

Then, last week, Elizabeth became the patient when she told me, "Sometimes my heart beats very fast and I have chest pain!

Neither an EKG nor a chest x-ray showed anything wrong and a visiting doctor felt it might be due to stress. At eighteen, she was married and had three children less than five years of age. She told me her husband was a good man but could only work intermittently because of back pain. So they were often hungry, she said. Her children were usually filthy and barefoot.

As the doctor spoke to her about his findings, I studied her. She had not recently bathed and wore ragged jeans and T-shirt. Her long hair was dirty, uncombed, and gathered messily into a clip. Yet she was stunning, a petite and flawless face on smooth mocha skin. When she smiled, as she often did, her perfect white teeth and dark eyes gleamed.

I asked her if she had experienced anything lately that might have caused her anxiety.

"Well, yes, my mother died three weeks ago."

She said it mildly, as though her loss were not worthy of attention. I translated for the doctor, then with a few gentle questions, a much larger story unfolded.

"She took care of me since I was a baby. My blood-mother abandoned me when I was seven-months old. Later she came back and took me with her but she sold me to men. She beat me so I wouldn't tell anyone. When my second mother finally came for me, I was almost dead from a very bad beating."

Besides her inner wounds, one leg was a patchwork of scars.

"What happened here?" I asked.

"They poured coffee on me and she would not let anyone take me to the hospital."

She still saw her biological mother when she visited her brother.

"I have forgiven her because I know that's what Jesus wants. Once I asked her to forgive me."

"For what?"

"Well, I know she will not ask me to forgive her and the Bible says it is better to give than to receive. Well, it just seemed like a good thing to do."

"It was an amazing thing to do, Elizabeth," I said with tears. "God is using you in powerful ways!"

She lowered her eyes.

"I miss my mother so much. She always helped me and prayed for me! "

I held her like the child she was and let her cry. When her sobbing eased, I told her, "I would love to be your friend, to be here for you if you ever want to talk or to have someone pray for you. You can come here anytime, or someday we'll get your husband to babysit and we'll go out for lunch. Okay?"

She smiled a smile that could have graced the cover of "Vogue" magazine. Then I offered up every prayer a mother would ask for her hurting daughter - for comfort, protection, strength, faith, power and love.

A week later, she came back. She sat in the busy waiting room while Joy tended her father's wound.

Though she said nothing, I noticed her and saw her seeking me with her eyes.

"Let me finish with this one patient and then you can come in, okay?" I told her.

As soon as possible, I ushered her into a quiet room and sat with her. It took me a few questions to get her to speak of her inner state, but soon she convinced me she was, indeed, better. Then she interrupted our conversation for something on her heart.

"Hermana, I want to tell you something! Last week when you told me you wanted to be my friend and pray for me, it made me very happy! I went home and thanked God because I knew He was taking care of me. That was the first time in my life anyone said that! No one ever told me she wanted to be my friend. You are the first, and I know you are from God."

When I recovered from the horrible shock that this lovely creature had never had a friend, the richness of what God had done filled me like a treasure. In the crazy marvelous mathematics of God, I felt more blessed than she.

Such simple words, how many times have we said them – "If you need anything, call! I'm here if you want to talk!" But when the Spirit of the Lord moves in, multiplying our loaves and fishes, miracles happen. People get fed. And I, like the disciples, got to watch in amazement as God took the measly and made it divine.

April 11, 2008

Ofelia, a houseparent at the orphanage, and I had a very special lunch date with Modesta, the mother of Esteban. At her son's funeral I'd promised her we'd come back in a month to take her out to lunch. By then we knew most of the well-wishers and supporters would have faded away and she'd need encouragement.

Our friend took the day off from work and we headed out to "Baja Gardens," a newly renovated restaurant in San Quintin.

"Have you eaten here?" I asked Ofelia. "It's really good!"

Ofelia said she had not but named other restaurants in the area she liked. There was an awkward pause. Should I ask one person about her dining preferences and not the other? Yet it would be like asking, "So, Modesta, do you prefer to vacation in the Bahamas, Europe, or somewhere else?" At a loss, I went ahead and asked if she had gone to any restaurants in the area and got the expected reply.

"No, hermana."

Partly because I've gotten so used to making a fool of myself and partly because I knew Modesta was too gracious to judge me, the moment passed. Quickly we were just three chicks having lunch. Well, there was one more clumsy moment when the waitress brought the menus. Ofelia and I started talking about the options while Modesta scanned hers quickly, closed it and set it back on the table. She couldn't read.

Ofelia got it before I did and told her, "They have meat, fish, shrimp," and so on. Modesta half-listened then told the waitress she'd have whatever I did. Thankfully, I'd splurged and ordered *Camarones Rancheros* instead of a Caesar salad.

Surely this mother was still mourning the loss of her special child but in this culture it was not common to share one's heaviest emotions. Heavy burdens were part of life. But we coaxed Modesta to enjoy the intimacy of women. She shocked us with an update on her family.

"My husband came back after Esteban's funeral."

"What do you mean, "came back? He visited you after the service?"

"He's living with me and the children again," she explained.

Wow! The man had abandoned them four years ago when the twins were two. He took off to live with another woman and left his wife with five kids, one severely handicapped, and no money. Modesta said she had cried and asked him over and over, "How can you leave me like this? What will I do?"

She had figured it out, though. Not only had she survived but she'd grown into an amazing saint, working hard, providing for her family, and still managing to give meticulous care to a completely-dependent son. Now her husband had waltzed back in.

Modesta knew we were stunned and she was smiling. I blurted out my questions.

"How is your relationship? Is he treating you well?"

I loved her answer. It was what any woman in the U.S. might say after reuniting with her deadbeat husband.

"Well, it's okay, but it's different now. I am not the same! He left and I had to do everything on my own, so it's not easy to have him there, but it's good for the children. We'll see."

"Well, yeah! For sure! He should respect you for all you've accomplished!" I replied. "He best treat you like a queen!"

She told us how touched he was by all that the "Christians" had done for his family. They had built them a new home and helped in so many ways with Esteban. Most importantly, he knew it was Christ Who had strengthened, empowered, comforted and transformed his wife. He didn't understand it completely, but he was going to church with her because this kind of love puzzled and attracted him.

"Praise the Lord, Modesta!" we yelled.

She was shyly thrilled at our exuberance and we three unlikely lunch-mates felt the joy of one Spirit. We left the restaurant hugging each other and laughing like children.

Ellie, Ofelia, Modesta

May 9, 2008

The stories of Big José and Little José began about the same time. Papa José was a short twenty-seven year old man who, a few months ago, sought rehabilitation from drugs. He entered the mission's offsite rehab program, Rancho de Cristo, and later shared that his nine-year old son had Muscular Dystrophy. Through the wonderful entanglement of the many arms of the mission, little José started attending the day-home for disabled children where he blossomed from shy and quiet to a high-spirited lovable clown.

Dad, meanwhile, also did well: cleaned up from drugs and sin, and enjoying life in Jesus. Then five weeks ago, he came to the clinic with a painful abscess in a tender area. Dr. Avitia ordered strong antibiotics, including three injections, which I administered daily with prayer.

Tuesday, José came back, complaining of increased pain and infection. Dr. Laura, a visiting doctor, saw him one day and Dr. Avitia followed the next. After deep intramuscular injections, a painful lancing and surgical exploration of the "tender" area, this "man-of-the streets" looked about as tough as his nine-year old son.

I had assisted Dr. Avitia with the surgery and was preparing a dressing when José said softly, "Hermana Ellie?"

"Yes?"

"How can I ever repay you?"

The words had less impact than his expression. He looked at me without a shred of pride or self-protection, a place of gratitude for all that life had given him lately. Physical illness, received correctly, can teach and transform. It can lay open hearts like Dr. Avitia's scalpel did the wound, draining any ridiculous sense of independence and turning us into children.

> *"...I tell you the truth, unless you change and become like little children, you will never enter the kingdom of heaven."* (Matt. 18:3)

"How can I ever repay you?" he repeated.

Because I hadn't answered, he thought I hadn't understood. The truth was, rather, I didn't know what to say. The depth of emotion in his eyes showed me that he'd confused me with Christ; I'd done nothing to merit such thankfulness. Laying there so vulnerable - in that humble childlike state - he had received the kingdom of heaven. He grasped how deeply his life had been changed and that his son also was receiving the blessings. He did not yet appreciate it was all the grace of God.

"Never do drugs again and grow stronger and stronger in Christ!" I told him. "That's my pay."

He smiled a sweet smile and promised to do so.

Later, the Lord reminded me it was okay, indeed, good, to be confused with Christ. It's our goal as Christians. Not so we can receive glory that we don't deserve, but that people will *"see our good deeds and praise our Father in heaven."* (Matt. 5:16)

This purposeful case of mistaken identity is called Christianity.

Little José

Papa José

May 18, 2008

Friday was my day to write so I was not in the clinic. People knew where to find me though, and they called me for a burnt foot, a catheter insertion, and several phone calls. This was part of my identity as "Nurse Ellie" and I loved it. By noon, however, when I saw Elizabeth's husband waiting outside my apartment with two of his children, I made him wait. My brother was getting married the next day and we were talking long-distance, a conversation I did not want to cut short.

When I finally opened the door, I was surprised to see the family without Elizabeth.

"Octavio! What's going on?"

This simple greeting made him cry.

"Elizabeth's run off with another man! She's drinking and partying! I told her if she repents, I will forgive her, but she said she doesn't want to come back!"

It was hard for me to think. I felt nauseated and heavy, betrayed.

"What?! No way!" was all that came out. Not my precious Elizabeth!

He followed with the details, including her negligence of her own children, physical abuse toward him, and lots of running around at night.

"I don't know where she is! She has the baby and she left me with these two older ones."

We talked a long time and prayed. I could think of little practical advice except to trust God and take care of the children, who kept fighting and crying. I wrote a note asking her to visit me and he said he'd try to get it to her.

The next few days she was the focus of my prayers but I was angry at her for abandoning her family. Then, one morning I went for a long walk on the beach, where God talked sense into me.

"Her wounds are too deep for human love to heal," the Lord whispered. "She needs divine love!"

With that, my anger vanished. God's love and mercy returned and I vowed to pray for her anew, with compassion. Octavio was a good husband, a faithful Christian man who adored her, but she had no understanding of such love – to her love was pain. So, of course, she ran.

Yesterday we had a surgery day in the clinic open to all. A three-year old boy had a benign cyst just above his right eyebrow. He screamed and fought during most of the surgery and it took three people to hold him down and try to soothe him. I was not involved with his case but was assisting Dr. Avitia with a different procedure in the same operating room. When, suddenly, his cries stopped, the silence shocked everyone. I looked over at the other table and saw that the little patient had fallen asleep! Everyone in the O.R. was smiling and surprised and the surgery finished in peace.

Elizabeth was like that child, I thought, frightened by the Lord's love and the very people who could help her. My prayer was that she would get tired of running and fighting, that she'd find rest in the midst of the surgery she so desperately needed. Then God would be able to do His exquisite work, reducing her scars and returning her to her anxious family.

It's an elective procedure. Please pray that Elizabeth comes back to her Lord and Healer while He can still save her family!

Tales of A Five-Star Missionary

In Happier Times

June 4, 2008

Lucero is fifteen months old. Already she's had surgery for Cleft Lip, placement of ear tubes, numerous ear infections, seven pneumonias, a bone marrow biopsy, and a feeding tube inserted into her stomach. Through all this, her caregiver Betty calls her "the most peaceful child on earth."

Lucero, the China doll

Abnormal lab results, frequent infections, and severe weight loss started a marathon of doctors' visits and hospitalizations. Her caregivers, Phil and Betty, had made twenty-eight trips to Ensenada or Tijuana, three and five hour drives from the mission.

Recently Phil went to visit family in the States so I drove Betty and the baby to Tijuana. Betty sat in the backseat so she could manage Lucy's tube feedings while we traveled. The baby hummed and gurgled a sweet song of comfort while being fed.

Nana Betty and Lucy off to TJ

The first week we visited a maxillofacial surgeon who was on time, pleasant, and welcomed questions.
"This place is great!" I remarked to Betty.
She smiled and said nothing.
Week two. We waited four hours for a hematologist who never showed. Around the waiting area, a stark beige place in the hospital basement, sat several children with Leukemia and their mothers. Most of the kids were bald from chemotherapy or wore face masks to protect their weakened immune systems.
One doctor had called Lucero "pre-leukemic" which made this more personal.
The next few hours we learned much: first, that this place was not just for waiting. These mothers knew one another – intimately. They shared facts and feelings, struggles and victories. When a two-year-old cried having his IV started, the pain on each mother's face was the same.

Without warning, another little boy vomited. His shirt and pants were soiled and a big puddle landed on the floor. No one looked surprised and three women helped clean him. The compassion of women is expected; the compassion of children, angelic. The sickest of all those we saw seemed to be a thin pale boy about six years old. He was bald and wore a cap and big dark glasses; probably the chemo had made him light sensitive. He watched for a while then walked over with more tissue.

"You have to clean his mouth," he said, handing the paper to the mom.

He spoke softly, his voice as weak as his body. But he knew something important: grownups clean your clothes and the floor after you vomit when what you really want is for someone to clean your mouth. More than the courage and unity of these mothers, more than the tragedy of kids with cancer, this act of compassion shown to one sick child by another tore my heart to pieces.

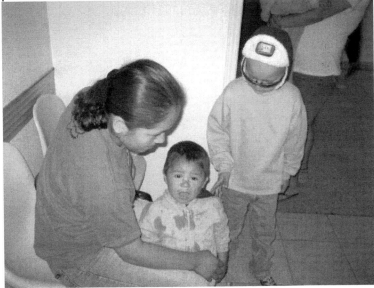

Lucero, meanwhile, smiled and reached out to the plump bald boy beside her. He resisted for a while but finally surrendered a smile and took her hand. She is delicate with huge joyful eyes, like a beautiful China doll.

Our hematologist never showed up. Another doctor examined her.

"She's fine, no problem," his assessment.

"The other doctor was worried about her blood tests," Betty said.

"Oh, well, I don't have them. Why don't you come back tomorrow?"

"We live five hours away," I told him.

"Okay, then draw new labs and come back next week."

Week three - my excitement made the drive easy. We were scheduled to meet with Dr. Guerra, a hematologist who had promised to look at Lucero's blood himself. Betty, veteran of twenty-seven such excursions, did not share my enthusiasm. "

"Dr. Guerra does not work here anymore,"

Marta, the woman who organized the department greeted us with the news. Our favorite specialist had disappeared into the black hole known as healthcare for the poor. The news took us to a new level of dismay, but we held our mouths. Our disappointment seemed trivial compared to those around us. Each of these children had a relationship with his doctor. Dr. Guerra always teased and comforted and greeted his patients. But now the doctor and hospital had divorced, and the little ones would suffer most.

Their mothers stayed united. They asked questions, comforted their young, and waited. Not one of them yelled, demanded, or put themselves ahead of the others. They bore this new bomb with patient endurance. We watched in awe.

We left with nebulous news – to come back in two days and one or another hematologist would see us. Maybe it would happen; likely not. But we were learning it was not our circumstances that matter; it was how we responded in those circumstances. On our long drive home, winding around and over the mountains, we helped each other to choose to rejoice. God was sovereign. He had not fallen asleep. That alone was exhilarating. But little children with cancer and their heroic mothers had brought us into a holy place. We would have been fools to despair or even complain after watching humans who chose to act like Christ.

Thirty trips to Mexican hospitals teach you patient endurance. Baby Lucero, unfazed and serenading us with her gurgle, looked pleased at our progress. We could not have found a better teacher.

Tales of A Five-Star Missionary

June 22, 2008

Whether you're a parent or working in an orphanage, it's probably wrong to have a favorite child. Still, certain ones just make your heart lurch with love and Miguel does that to mine. Some of you will remember him from Christmastime when he rejected me as surrogate mom. Since then a lot has happened.

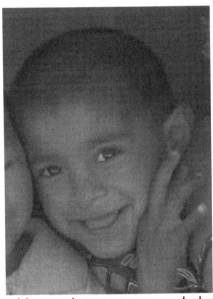

Paula, his real mom, moved back to Baja. Drought had made for a slow tomato season and she, like many, had moved out of state to find work. The decision to leave Miguel at the orphanage was based on his need for Cleft Palate surgery in February. She always planned to return but his three-year-old mind and heart could not understand. He felt abandoned so, indeed, he was. Miguel told us with sign language that his father had beaten his mom and made her cry. After another baby was born, the dad ran off with another woman. Therefore, to Miguel, mom's going away felt like a second parent abandonment.

Heavy winter rains in Baja produced abundant strawberry crops and jobs for pickers. Paula returned with a new boyfriend and Miguel's two siblings. She moved into a filthy camp near the mission and showed up one day to take her son back.

"He's recovered from his surgery!" Mary told me. "The only reason for him to stay at the mission now would be for school, and because we love him! But his mom loves him, too. We can not say no!"

He went gladly. Paula asked if he could continue to go to school.

"We can pick him up and bring him home every day," Mary and Dirk told her.

The first week was tough. He screamed and cried most of the day, but once he understood he would go home each afternoon, he changed.

"You wouldn't believe how good Miguel is now!" Mary said. "His anger is gone! He is such a sweet little boy! He doesn't fight like before; he minds the teacher and almost never needs a time out. Such a difference!"

Everyone noticed. Miguel was still Miguel, who could charm and clown his way into anyone's heart, but the angry outbursts were gone. He had peace.

Last week his mom asked Betty if a nurse could visit a sick baby in the camp. We drove there, opened a tin gate and walked into Dogpatch. It was impossible to tell where one family's quarters ended and another's began. Tin walls created a few dark rooms here and there, but mostly, things you would expect to see in kitchens or living rooms were just stacked on shelves in the dirt under blue tarp roofs. No flooring, no walls.

Miguel and his sister were watching mom pluck the last remaining feathers out of a dead chicken. He ran over and greeted us with delight, unaware of my dismay.

To see anyone in such poverty was sad; to see my precious Miguel filthy, barefoot, and at home here was ghastly. Two flea-infested dogs had passed their pests onto him; his legs bled from his scratching. There was no bathroom or running water and a worn-out couch, turned on its side, served as a playhouse for him and his friends. With all this, what was hardest for me to accept was how happy he looked.

I thought back to Christmas when he lived at the mission. We'd kept him so clean and pampered! Bonnie and I had staggered his gifts over a week since he had so many. Our evening ritual was bath, story, Advent calendar, brushing his teeth, and prayer time. He slept in a toddler's bed with an oak frame. His sheets and comforter were a matched set, patterned with toy trains.

Now he and his family slept in one dark room. Whether he shared a bed with everyone or slept on a mat on the ground, I didn't know, but his life had changed like the crisis point of a classic novel. The part when the child is temporarily made to suffer in rags, filth, and hunger. The part before his real parents find him and take him back to their big beautiful house for the happy ending.

But for Miguel, the dirt, tin, fleas, and garbage *was* the happy ending. The mission, the day home, and all of us who adored him could not compete with what he had now. One huge difference transformed his heart, calmed his anger, and filled him with joy. The difference made by a mother's love.

Miguel at Christmas with presents

Miguel at home with his Family

July 12 2008

This story has to be written for two reasons. One is to correct wrong information I gave out about Elizabeth. The second is to speak out for all the abused women in Mexico, a huge majority.

In May, when Octavio came to my door crying and accusing Elizabeth of unfaithfulness and abandonment, I took him at his word. When she showed up two days later, she brought two policemen from the Domestic Violence Bureau in San Quintin and a much different story than her husband's.

"He hit Genesis (the oldest daughter) and made her nose bleed! I went out to call the police, and when I came back, he was gone. He has my children!"

She denied having an affair and said her husband had been controlling and beating her for years. They married when he was almost thirty and she, only thirteen. This is the age when many Oaxacan Indian women are sold by their fathers. The usual price for a virgin is three thousand dollars and a case of beer. *Usadas* or "used" women cost half.

Various people have since confirmed that they've witnessed Octavio's anger, directed at mission workers and at his children.

Meanwhile, one woman after another came to the clinic with a menagerie of body aches and disturbances. Headaches, stomach aches, heartburn, general malaise, and the all-too-common *"No tengo fuerzas,"* (I don't have any strength.) I learned they could all be signs of a battered spirit. Yet abuse was so common and accepted here. What could I tell these sisters of mine?

I told them that I had been in an abusive relationship for three years and that I understood the loneliness, heartache, and degradation. I offered them a three-day refuge if they ever felt unsafe and told them we'd help them find long-term lodging.

"Just because it is accepted by some, doesn't mean it is right! Abuse is sin! It is wrong in the eyes of God and very dangerous."

This was important to say because if all your neighbors are eating poisonous snakes, you might not know there's a better diet. Each one got prayer but still, I felt overwhelmed. The women had to go home. They had no job, plenty of kids, no skills and, often, no other family.

Then God sent me Judy Perry. A counselor with twenty-five years of experience, she visited the mission and took me under her wing for a week. She gave me resources and encouragement.

"There is no magic answer, Ellie. Tell them your story, share their pain, educate them, and lead them to the Lord! And always pray!"

So, I was ready when a frail Indian woman came in, dark-skinned with a thick braid that reached her waist.

"My head hurts! It starts here," she said, holding the side of her face, "then it moves over here," touching her other cheek. By the time she listed four other hazy complaints, I asked about her marriage.

"Toma alcohol, grita mucho." He drinks and yells a lot.

"Le pega?" Does he hit you?

"Sí."

In his book, *The Bondage Breaker*, Neil Anderson wrote that "freedom from spiritual conflicts and bondage is not a power encounter; it's a truth encounter." He compares Satan's lies to cockroaches that run for the shadows when the light comes on. "We don't have to overpower the father of lies, we just have to "out-truth him!"

So I fed truth and light to this Christian woman.

"God designed a woman to be cherished, loved, protected, not abused. When you're abused you begin to believe lies; you think you're weak and alone! The truth, my sister, is that God has given women great power and never leaves us alone! I suggest you find two other married women, abused or not, and the three of you pray for your marriages. If you do this, God will work powerfully in your homes! You are not weak, Paula; you are a warrior fighting for yourself and your family!"

As she received truth and cast off lies, power shone from her eyes and gave strength to her whole being. When we prayed, it was just to praise the Lord for the already-assured victory.

God Himself made woman Satan's enemy in the Garden of Eden when she was the first to identify the serpent as a "deceiver." Genesis 3:15, *"I will put enmity between you and the woman,"* is a powerful statement. It gives me great hope for the battle to be waged against the exploitation and abuse of women that is out of control around the world. If we give these women knowledge and resources, we will empower them. If we lead them into relationship with Jesus and get them to pray in groups, we will change the world.

"You shall know the truth, and the truth shall set you free." (John 8:32)

July 18 2008

I've been having a crisis of faith lately. The decision to stay in Mexico came to me months ago without doubt or hesitation. God called me and the rest was simply details. But when I was about to announce my decision and ask for your continued support, I found myself spiraling down into a pit of uncertainty and depression.

Poverty is the issue. It's a term or rather, state of being, that is misunderstood. I used to think of it as a sort of ranking assigned to you by some bureaucrat when you don't have enough money. But enough money for what? Day after day here, I see people without enough money to buy food, without enough money for an antibiotic, without enough money to buy diapers, shoes, school supplies, water. These are material real needs but poverty also means not having enough money to have choices: to decide to leave a man who beats you, to decide whether to receive chemotherapy or die, to decide whether to get an education or work in the fields like a slave.

Yesterday a medical team went to a small community called Zapata for a free clinic. We set up in the storeroom of a small grocery store owned by a Christian family. Because we had not advertised well, we walked through the neighborhood inviting people to come for a *consulta gratis* (free medical consultation.) Many did. We saw the usual coughs and colds, aches and pains, diabetes, and skin problems caused by filth and dehydration. Some women came just to talk to someone who cared, certain children for something to do; but we believed God had sent each one.

The shopkeeper, Rosa, was middle-aged and had a smile that destroyed poverty. She had asked for prayer once in our church because her husband was unfaithful. So I asked her how things were going and she whispered, *"No muy bien, hermana."* Her husband lived at home but didn't speak to her and didn't even attempt to hide his current extra-marital affair. When she held her fist to her heart and cried, *"Me lastima!"* (it hurts me!), my descent began. The words of encouragement and faith I love to share with abused women seemed false, so we hugged in silence and shared her pain.

"Pray for me!" she pleaded, but I was glad to leave.

At home, my hot shower did nothing to wash away the grime I felt. Truthfully, neither did prayer. I kept my word to her, though, and prayed.

Sleep was fitful and by morning many concerns all led to one central question: do I belong here? The disrepair and lack of beauty in my apartment, indeed my life, kept me from getting out of bed. My thoughts were not lovely, *I hate my cramped cement shower, I hate my ugly mismatched linoleum, I hate not being able to buy decent groceries, I hate Rosa's husband for mistreating her and I really hate the hopeless state of women here.*

When my own deep poverty threatened to choke me and thoughts of escaping to my comfortable three-bedroom home lingered, I sought God. I ran to the chair where I pray and vowed, "Lord, I will not get up until You talk to me!" I prayed in silence then in cries and even some weak attempts at praise. Nothing. I grabbed my Bible, opened to where I had left off in Luke, expecting nothing.

But there it was.

"The kingdom of God does not come with your careful observation, nor will people say, 'Here it is,' or 'There it is,' because the kingdom of God is within you."

My focus shifted. The filth and poverty, the abuse, the temptations of comfort in my old life, all these were the "here" and "there." By the power of the word of God, I turned "within" and found the kingdom of God. Peace, joy, hope, self-control sparking within me, simply needing to be fanned back into flame.

Further down in Luke 17, I read, *"People were eating and drinking, buying and selling, planting and building."* And that was what I would do if I moved home. However, eating and shopping would not satisfy me now.

The Lord finished bringing me to my senses with Colossians 3:2-3.

"Set your mind on things above, not on earthly things. For you died and your life is now hidden with Christ in God."

"Set your mind on things above," not on the beach in Carlsbad, not on going to movies and restaurants, nor buying healthy food at "Jimbo's." None of that would quench my desire to serve God. But to struggle here with mothers who feed their starving kids too much sugar and battered wives who don't realize God wants to empower them, *that* will get me out of bed!

Praise the Lord for wisdom and clarity where there was none! Renewed and certain, I can now tell you I'm where I'm supposed to be. So when my year is up in October, it will mark a new beginning but not an end.

My heart fills with love and humility every time I consider what I have received from you in the past year. Never have I felt alone. God has shown His faithfulness through you and your faithfulness has shown me God.

His richest blessings and love,
Ellie

August 5, 2008

Sometimes Spanish flows out of my mouth with good grammar and ever-increasing vocabulary. Then I make a mistake that convinces me what happened at the Tower of Babel is irrevocable.

Years ago, when I knew even less of the language than now, I walked into a café in Puerto Vallarta to get a cup of tea. Someone had introduced me *to té de Manzanilla,* made from chamomile leaves and I wanted a cup to go. A common mistake made by those new to a language is to translate exactly as we think in our native tongue.

So I told the waitress, *"Yo quiero un Manzanilla té para ir!"*

Ir is the verb "to go" and *para* means "for, in order to" so I felt confident I'd ordered my drink "to go." The problem was Spanish-speakers don't say "to go" for takeout; they say "to carry" which is *para llevar.* So the waitress heard "to go" and "Manzanilla" and proceeded to tell me where I could catch a bus to Manzanillo, a beautiful town three hours south! Equally confused, we persevered and eventually I got my tea and we shared the laugh.

My most recent error occurred on a busy day in the clinic. A co-worker and I were talking with Regina, a small sturdy woman who had worked years in the local ranches and looked much older than her fifty-three years. She was Christian and sharing her faith with other believers lifted her spirit. However, she was distraught over her son-in-law's emotional abuse toward her daughter. The young couple and their gorgeous baby girl lived with her.

"He's mean to her and lazy, he only works once in a while," she told us. "I saved enough to put a down payment on a piece of land. María said she was going to leave him and move with me to the new property, but she's still with him. So we all live together in a *casa de cartones* on my land.

Cartones, was one case where the two languages were equivalent. The house was made of flattened cardboard boxes or "cartons."

"How does he treat you?" I asked.

"Cold, but not too bad because he knows I am the one who pays for everything. It will take six years to finish paying for the property. Right now what we need is a *lona.*

All this was, of course, in Spanish.

She clarified, *"Necesitamos una lona así que no tiene techo la casa."*

Oh, now I get it! I thought. Techo means roof so she was saying they needed a loan *(lona)* because the house had no roof. I wondered how much of a loan they needed. Things often cost much less down here. Maybe I could help them, but it would be tricky since handouts of anything - clothes, money, food – created unhealthy relationships. *And besides,* I thought, *a roof was probably beyond my resources.*

Later I asked Ingrid, "How much of a loan would she need?"

She laughed and explained, "No, Ellie, it isn't a loan she wants! She was asking for a *lona!* That means "tarp!" She wants to cover her house with it."

The next day we visited them and their carton house, in the middle of a huge field which had been divided into lots. The structure looked like it wouldn't withstand a Baja windstorm, let alone a winter rain. The current roof was made from palm fronds and a tarp would certainly decrease the invasion of dust and rain. They had no water, electricity, sewerage, nor a single piece of furniture. I imagined these two wonderful women could manage a life here with the baby; to share it with a lazy abusive man would turn it into a nightmare.

Since I could not get rid of José, I resolved to get them a tarp for my own peace of mind. I found one for a hundred pesos at the local hardware, about nine dollars, and delivered it with a bag of fruit.

Look at the photo below and tell me if you think I'll suffer from buyer's remorse.

August 29, 2008

Charla Pereau didn't have me in mind when she founded this mission forty-two years ago, but God did. I was thirteen then and Enrique Lugo, a Mexican boy, would have been only seven. The omniscient One saw that we would both make some poor choices in life and wander to a distant country, but that in the end, we would come to our senses and return to the Father's house. He used Charla to build a place where rejected children would be loved and the gospel of peace would be acted out in practical ways. Into that mix of blessings He threw in for Enrique and me to meet.

It happened last November and this man has opened something deep within me that I didn't know was closed. For the first time in my fifty-five years, I want to be someone's wife. I want to pray for this man, work beside him in ministry, respect him, listen to him, and yes, maybe even submit – the Lord does so many miracles!

As God loved me before I loved Him, Enrique did as well. And as the Lord gradually won my love by faithfully loving me, so Enrique told me, "I'm going to make you love me because no man is ever going to love you more than I do. You'll see!"

Romance is as natural for Latino men as sarcasm is for New Englanders. So when he tells me things like, "If I had two hearts I'd love you with both of them, but I only have one and it's yours." I smile and tell him he has a, *"lengua de oro!"* ("golden tongue!")

But daily he shows me the truth of his words, in patience, in thoughtfulness, and devotion.

This, however, is not what won me. Three characteristics did that: great inner strength, courage, and most important, an enormous love for God. Last Monday on the steps of the clinic, he got on his knees and asked me to marry him. In my usual decisive manner, with great excitement, I responded, "Probably!" (Fifty-five years of living for one's self is not easily relinquished.) But I have seen God's hand over and over in this relationship and as sure as I was that God called me to the orphanage, so now I am sure He is joining the two of us for His purpose.

So I said, "Yes!" and am as content and excited as any twenty-year old bride-to-be. With maybe one exception: I realize more than a twenty-year old how much I, (I mean, we) need your prayers.

Enrique still wants to complete the Bible School here which means two more years of classes followed by a year of service in Oaxaca. He has the voice of an angel and when he leads worship, the congregation enters the holy of holies. So his future will likely include the role of pastor and worship leader.

We have not set a date as a long paper trail awaits us first. The wedding will be in Mexico with all the children of the handicapped program as my attendants. Some of these were the first ones I told and when they see us together now, they tease us with, "Ellie! *Tu amor!*" pointing at Enrique. I nod my head and tell them, yes, but then assure them they are still my *otros amores,* (other loves) and they smile like angels.

God is amor and all amor comes from God. What a blessing to receive it in this new manner!

Engaged!

September 16 2008

Being a bride-to-be is a special honor. Everyone wants to share my excitement and sharing it increases my joy. Even strangers desire details about my beloved and our wedding. All this has blessed me with fresh appreciation of the church as Christ's bride-to-be.

Friday, I left Enrique in Tijuana and crossed into the States for the weekend. Everywhere I went friends celebrated my engagement and those who have known me the longest recognized the miracle. They wanted to hear descriptions of Enrique and I told of all the wonderful ways he showed me his love.

"Our first night out as a couple, we went to a dinner and matrimony conference. As we entered, Enrique spotted a friend of mine at a table with some empty seats."

"There's Angelina!" he told me. "Do you want to sit with her?"

"Yes!" I replied, and without waiting another breath, ran to claim two seats.

My fiancé arrived a moment later and whispered, "Ellie, can you try to remember you are part of a couple now? You went rushing off and left me!"

The threat of a controlling mate brought out a careless response.

"Well, yes, I'm part of a couple, but I'm not handicapped!"

We discussed it and finally he told me, "Look, Ellie, I'm just telling you what I'd like. You can do anything you want and I'm going to forgive you because I love you!"

"With such love, he won the argument. The next occasion, we entered as a couple."

My girlfriends laughed, knowing my independent ways, but telling the story reminded me of Enrique's great love.

Kathy, my maid-of-honor, shares my love for Christ and Mexico. Shopping together for a wedding dress was hilarious, but it held an unreal quality. There was this sense of being a character in a movie, a romantic comedy in which I should have been the doting mother, yet had somehow been cast as the bride.

"This is too low-cut for a missionary!" I commented on one gown.

"Oh, it looks great on you!" the owner replied. "But if you're uncomfortable, we can take it up from the shoulders. Where are you a missionary?"

We began to tell of the orphanage and all that God has done through it. Another bride-to-be overheard and joined the conversation.

"I'm in Bible School and some of our students need a place to serve next semester. That sounds perfect!"

We gave her the website of Foundation For His Ministry and shared stories of our fiancés and the Lord's work in our lives (not to mention getting a price discount when the shopkeeper heard "what good things we were doing!")

During these special days, I recognized what a privilege and honor Jesus has bestowed upon believers. Enrique won me by his faithful love and godly character. A certain restfulness mingled with joy comes from knowing I can trust him and depend on him. To have such a relationship heightened to perfection with the Lord of all creation is an exquisite gift.

God commands us to be evangelists because it is in the telling and description of his great Love that others believe and become part of the bride-to-be. And the telling infuses us with deeper love.

However, by Sunday morning, sharing stories and thinking ahead to the wedding weren't enough to satisfy my longing. I desired one thing above all: to be with my lover, to rush into his embrace and enjoy being together.

This, the symbol of the highest state of being we can attain on earth: to unite with Christ, to live in the fullness of His presence.

Enrique and I will become one on November twenty-second. Led by the Holy Spirit, we will help each other to be the best we can be in an imperfect world. The church, the spotless bride, will become one with her Savior at the wedding feast in heaven. It will be a perfect relationship because when we see our Husband face-to-face we will be like Him.

What a romantic God we have! Let the marriage begin!

Mexican Independence Day

September 28 2008

Last week a group of us from the clinic attended a conference in Pasadena. The West Coast Healthcare Missions Conference presented us with a fresh vision of health ministry.

First some sad facts:
1. Forty thousand children die daily of diseases which could have been prevented. Of these, ninety-eight percent occur in developing countries.
2. Curative medicine has been available for years, but worldwide, people who live in rural areas are not getting healthier.
3. Over half the preventable deaths of children are related to malnutrition and infection (diarrhea, gastrointestinal diseases caused by contaminated water and food, improper waste disposal, poor hygiene, and poor nutrition.)
4. When health services are received by villagers, they are mostly curative, but 80% of their disease problems are preventable through health education and vaccines.

Many of the Lord's best healthcare providers now humbly admit we have not served the poor in the most excellent way. We have flown into their villages for two weeks, told them what *we* thought they needed, handed out drugs like candy and left. Infections returned, drugs caused unmonitored harmful side effects, and the transformation of lives was not top priority.

"Hope deferred makes the heart sick," says Proverbs 13:12, *"but a longing fulfilled is a tree of life."*

God is bringing miraculous transformation to the global poor through people with vision. Many speakers told us the same thing.

"We are educating people in what causes diseases and how they can maintain health. We train healthcare workers to teach and provide care within their communities, and now the people have hope."

"We ask people about their greatest needs and help them find ways to meet those needs, even if it is different than our assessment."

My favorite story came from a missionary in Uganda.

"In a community where the incidence of AIDS was 26%, a survey asked the local people to name their community's biggest problem. Unanimously, they answered, "We have no soccer field!"

In humility and with respect for those they were serving, the mission team helped the locals raise the money and worked together to build a soccer field. When it was completed, one of the town's elders came to them with a welcome request, "Can you help us with our AIDS problem?"

Trust had been established, and God's way of doing things bore fruit.

Missionaries are learning to empower, respect and love the poor. The change is bringing hope, the greatest medicine of all time.

So this Thursday, while two doctors attended patients at an outreach, I spoke to the children about germs. Using poster-sized drawings from our Health Education Program for Developing Countries (hepfdc.org) and my ability to act ridiculous in a way kids enjoy, we learned that sneezing and then shaking hands can spread disease. We sang *Feliz Cumpleaños* to a girl while washing our hands to demonstrate the length of time recommended to perform the task.

The children listened and responded with enthusiasm. During fourteen years of working in an Intensive Care Unit, I never felt so fulfilled.

To God be the glory!

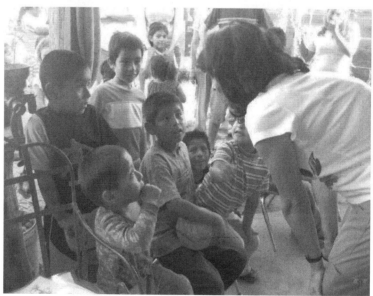

October 12, 2008

Javier is so weak from Muscular dystrophy that he can not stand up or cough hard enough to clear his lungs. He's thirteen and growing tall, but not gaining weight. His frame is nothing but sticks and protuberances, his features, especially the perfect white teeth, look too large for his face. His faith, however, is ten times stronger than mine.

The boy is a tireless fountain of joy. Every morning as someone pushes his wheelchair towards sala, he hollers out greetings to all his friends, and to strangers.

It is a treat to hear him yell, "Ellie!" whether or not my door is open.

I answer him, *"Buenos días, Javier!"* and these days he asks, "Tu amor?"

This means he wants to know where Enrique is because, of course, they have become friends, too.

In *sala*, he sings loud and off key. His favorite song is *"Alaba a Dios!"* (Praise God!) a beautiful song about praising God always, even in the midst of sickness, suffering, or silence. I wonder if he understands how exquisitely he lives out the mandate.

My heart sorrows to watch the effort it takes for him to move his arms. Sometimes I'll hold my hand near his so we can clap to the music. With a big grin, he inhales more deeply, shrugs his shoulders to help move one arm closer to the other. Then he uses that hand to grab the opposite wrist and lift it up to meet mine. When he swings the open palm towards mine, it's a sweet victory.

Javier is rarely downcast or negative. So what happened the other night at Dirk and Mary's was startling. Due to a high fever, they'd kept him overnight for monitoring.

At dinner, Dirk said, "Come on, Javier, eat up! If you want to be strong and healthy, you have to eat, like me!"

Then he flexed his muscles and roared. Javier laughed in delight.

He said, "Papa Cate (Dirk's nickname) *muy fuerte* (very strong.)"

"Sí," answered Dirk.

Then, in a quiet voice, he spoke two words of heart-wrenching truth.

"Yo, no." (I'm not.)

It was the first time we'd heard him so discouraged and it cut us to the core. But he did not linger in sadness, for Javier has chosen to spend his short life in joy.

I am also weak. I am unable to stand the long lines of bureaucracy blocking the way to my wedding. When we drove to Ensenada for the third time to pick up our final papers, a young official told us,

"They are all complete. Except..."

The "exception" was that they had put Enrique's name on a payment receipt instead of mine. We had questioned them at the time but were told it didn't matter. It was not one of the official documents, only a statement from the bank. But now began a four hour labyrinth of time, frustration, and paperwork. Partly because he is more familiar with Mexican "officialdom" and partly because he is my spiritual superior, Enrique recognized my bad attitude early on and tried to correct it.

"Ellie, we have to praise God for this! He's in control and He is so good to us!"

Pouting, I said, "Well, I've been praying for patience but He's not giving it to me."

"Come on, Ellie, you know better than that! You think you ask for patience and He's going to go 'Poof!'

and give it to you? No, it's in these circumstances we grow to trust Him and be patient!"

In this honeymoon phase of our relationship, I saw he was utterly right. As hard as it was for Javier, so it was for me, but I determined to start clapping to the music.

"Bless this woman and her family, her finances, her computer skills!"

This was my honest prayer for the woman who tried for an hour to change the mistake by Internet.

"Lord, I give you my life, my will, my circumstances – not just generally, but here and now, today!"

Over and over I renewed my mind, chasing away thoughts like forcing someone to sign our papers at gunpoint. At the end of the day I would have given myself a "D" - the grade you get when you fail miserably but at least made some effort.

The Lord kept reminding me about Javier. When I went to prayer, He showed me more clearly why.

"When your weak little darling child tries to clap, you wish with all your heart that you could give him power! Well, when I see you, one of my many weak darlings, try to do one good thing for My sake, I will certainly not laugh at your feebleness! It blesses me just as much as if you had done it perfectly, maybe more."

So I look at Javier and his spiritual generosity and marvel. He is so strong. Yo, no.

But my God says to me,

"My grace is sufficient for you, for my power is made perfect in weakness.' Therefore I will boast all the more gladly about my weaknesses, so that Christ's power may rest on me. That is why, for Christ's sake, I delight in weaknesses, in insults, in hardships, in persecutions, in difficulties. For when I am weak, then I am strong."

It is as difficult for me to raise my hand as it is for Javier to raise his, but we lift them high and gladly sing, "Alaba a Dios!"

Dirk (Papa Cate), Javier, and Feliciano

November 4, 2008

In an effort to empower local communities to prevent disease, we are giving health classes to women and children. Poster-size drawings and simple language keep the kids' attention. The information in the "Health Education Program for Developing Countries" is the best available and comes from such experts as World Health Organization and Center for Disease Control.

"Who knows what germs are?" I asked a small group of dirty but adorable children.

"They're little animals you can't see," said the oldest girl.

I praised her for her correct response. Padre Kino was a filthy migrant camp. The residents lived in a motel-style structure around a communal dirt yard, strewn with litter, mangy dogs, and drying laundry.

Leyde, the missionary in charge of the outreach, told us, "This camp is a great place to talk about hygiene. It's so dirty!"

We sat the children on a tarp. I taught them how germs are passed and why hand washing was so important.

"When should we wash our hands?"

With help from the poster, they answered, "Before you eat, after going to the bathroom, when you cough."

Near the end of the presentation, a tiny toddler walked by, fascinated by what he had in his hand.

"Is that a mouse dangling from his grasp?" I asked myself. *"No, it must be a toy!"*

I went on about the benefits of soap and water.

But one of the visitors who had come with us approached me and whispered, "Ellie, that little boy has a dead mouse in his hand!"

In life we have priorities. We organize our day around what we consider these priorities to be, but 9/11 or more minor catastrophes cause us to reconsider continually. The child with the deceased rodent shifted my focus.

"Put that down, honey, it's dirty!" I said, shaking little Mickey out of his hand.

With a few gentle kicks, I transported the mouse to a corner then used a shovel to pick it up and deposit it in the trash. Two men, sitting on upside-down plastic buckets in front of their quarters, watched me with little interest. Apparently, a baby with a dead animal was not cause for action.

Too late, I turned back to the unruffled boy who was now sucking on the same pudgy fingers that had just held the mouse. In helpless horror I watched him.

Just then a large dog walked over to the clothesline. A double bed-sheet was dragging on the ground and the mutt sprayed it with urine. As happens so often down here, the dirt and dust and filth started to choke me, physically, emotionally, spiritually.

But having completed one year here, I recover more quickly than before. Any earthly standards I may once have used to measure what is good have been discarded. What are my priorities - teaching hand washing to ten or twelve kids, grabbing a dead mouse away from a two-year old, or simply to obey God's command to love and help the poor? If it's not this last one, then I am giving out dry crumbs instead of Living Water. We are not in the business of social change alone, thank God! We seek nothing less than complete transformation of lives, our own and others', through the demonstration and power of a living, paying-attention God.

From the tiniest germ to apathetic fathers to the heart and soul of every child on earth, *nothing* is out of His control. He teaches us to see what is needed and in our frailty, we reach out to help. From this point on, the missionary *has* to trust that the true Gardener will produce much fruit from his seeds.

"Apart from me you can do nothing" (John 15:5b)

"Now to Him Who is able to do immeasurably more than all we ask or imagine, according to His power that is at work within us, to Him be glory in the church and in Christ Jesus throughout all generations, for ever and ever! Amen." (Eph. 3:20-21)

December 12, 2008

I am a wife. Few can grasp how odd that sounds to my ears, let alone my being, after fifty-five years alone. But my husband shows me new love each day and in so many ways, reflects God's boundless devotion. Though billions of wives have been cherished, I feel uniquely blessed.

When separate beings unite in love, something divine and mystical occurs. Our wedding, if I may say, was glorious. The church shone with red and white floral bouquets, yards of white tulle, and the chairs elegantly draped. So many people helped with the preparation it felt like ancient days when a whole town took on the task of preparing for a wedding. After weeks of delegating tasks and resolving problems, we celebrated not as a couple but as part of a very special community; our joy spilling out and given back.

And how the children blessed the day and brought their special holiness down the aisle! We changed the normal order of procession so I could be there to receive each of my darlings.

First, Enrique received me. The congregation saw a simple gesture of him taking my hand; only I saw the passion and welcome in his gaze.

Then we turned and waited as each child approached us, most in wheelchairs or using walkers. Brenda, having practiced for the wedding, walked without her walker for the first time, and few knew how special she felt.

Muscular Dystrophy, Spina Bifida, Osteogenesis Imperfecta, Cerebral Palsy – these are the names of the diseases which had robbed our precious friends of normal physical abilities. But on this day, the infirmities did not exist. As Brenda, Javier, Feliciano, Jose, Luis, Alexis, Ariana, darling Miguel, Lupita, Rosita, Maria, Stefanie, Domitila, Zaida, Cristian, and Sandra came toward me, all I saw was the child (or woman, in the case of Sandra) that I loved.

The girls wore beautiful dresses and bands of flowers on their heads. Each boy had on a smart white shirt, dark pants, with a single red rose on his collar. Zaida had had surgery on her legs only two weeks earlier so she, too, walked for the first time with no aid. With her joy I forgot to even notice her gait.

One after the other hugged and kissed me; I thought Miguel's wild embrace might knock off my tiara, but how sweet was each reception!

So Jesus will receive us one day as His bride. And so, too, will we come to Him, not as wounded, imperfect children, but utterly and perfectly transformed through His gaze of divine love.

It continually amazes me how Enrique sees my flaws and loves me, not in spite of, but somehow, for them. As our God of grace sees us in all our sins and failings and loves us unto death.

If I died tomorrow, it would have been worth getting married to know this kind of love, of my husband, of these extraordinary, wonderful children, and of a God who longs for the day when we can be one with Him! Knowing such love exists makes me eager for all to join in. Share with me this Christmas season the joy of Emmanuel, God with us! Now and forever, be joined to His love.

Merry Christmas!
Ellie and Enrique

"For this reason, a man shall leave his father and mother and be united to his wife, and the two shall become one flesh. This is a profound mystery – but I am talking about Christ and the church." (Ephes. 5:31-32)

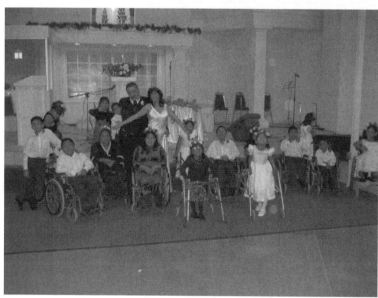

2009

January 5, 2009

As my plane began its descent over the Boston suburbs, I pressed my face into the windowpane. The roads far below us wound through bare woods and snowy fields. Under grey skies, wintry Massachusetts appeared as a black-and-white photograph. I tried to recognize the places we flew over, secluded towns of my youth now wealthy extensions of the city.

New England without snow doesn't feel like Christmas so I was pleased they'd had a heavy recent storm. Snow fell now like God's grace, in a soft and silent manner, covering everything. It was the only real beauty in an otherwise stark and frozen landscape. As I watched, I pondered how people respond in like ways to divine grace as they do to snow. Some fight it, even curse it. Others notice it, and then shovel it away into useless piles so they can get on with their business. Only children and those with childlike hearts, those to whom the kingdom of God belongs, simply receive it. They marvel at its magic, delight in its purity, lie down in wonder, enjoying it exactly as our Father intended.

***

Now I am home - my new home, with my husband in Baja. It was hard to leave my parents and siblings, nieces and nephews on the East Coast under snow, but I take comfort in knowing they are also under grace. God is with them and He is here, with good works that He prepared in advance for us to do. So pray that we will all receive what the Lord intends, especially the poor of the San Quintin Valley.

This year we will receive training in "Community Health Evangelism," a worldwide vision born out of the recognition that what we have been doing doesn't work. Medical missionaries have trekked and flown into the most remote areas of the world donating tons of medicines, clothing, and supplies. They have built houses, done surgery, handed out Bibles. Yet experts who reviewed the statistics were humble enough to admit: overall health and quality of life did not improve, people showed little desire to help themselves, and they did not grow spiritually.

Community Health Evangelism (CHE) was designed as a strategy to empower and equip the poor to improve their own lives and therefore, their communities. It is holistic and follows the example of Jesus in which a person's whole being is honored and addressed, the physical, emotional, and spiritual. It is humble and meets people in their own felt needs, as Jesus did. This will be our focus of the new year, a vision that will unite all areas of the mission in one goal based on the model of Christ's love and healing. Please pray for successful implementation and that God's grace may be received by His children, in New England, Mexico, and around the world.

Tales of A Five-Star Missionary

January 16, 2009

I don't know who this story's about. At first I thought it was Rosa, a student at the Bible Institute who is so mature in Christ my mind refuses to believe she's only seventeen. The day began with her preaching in sala.

"Psalm one tells us the righteous will avoid those who are wicked, will not keep company with sinners. Instead, they will find their pleasure in the word of God, meditating on it day and night."

She was beautiful, with great almond-shaped eyes, her black hair blown stick straight, and smartly dressed. A serene confidence showed that the Lord was speaking through her.

"As soon as I graduate I want to go back and finish high school then go to nursing school," she told me. "I think being a nurse will be a great way for me to reach people with the message of Jesus."

Since she was serving in the clinic when she revealed this to me, I began to include her in more nursing activities. Yesterday we went to Jose Dolores, a poor community where we were doing a series of health education classes for women. Two other nurses, Lynda and Lorna, came with us in the small car. They were both long-term visitors from Canada, and also whom this story is about. They were close to my age and we took joy like three mothers over our teenager's excitement to go out and serve the Lord.

The lesson was on the importance of breastfeeding and how to prevent and treat diarrhea in babies. Lynda was an obstetrical nurse, sharing valuable information with the young mothers. Rosa took it all in like she was gorging at an all-you-can-eat.

"I didn't know that breastfeeding could help prevent infections and diarrhea and make you grow up more intelligent! Wow! Too bad my mother bottle-fed me!"

"Believe me, Rosa, you've made up for it." I told her. "God has given you more wisdom than you could get from any milk!"

She "got" that these women were being empowered through knowledge and thrilled to see this manner of developing relationships while holding up the name of Christ.

But it was our next visit where we experienced God's miraculous coincidences. Paulina, an elderly woman, was dying of cancer. Her son and daughter-in-law had come to the clinic asking for a hospital bed and we told them we would first make a visit. The lady's entire body was swollen, her legs and arms too heavy to move by herself, her face stretched and unrecognizable. Weakly conscious, suffering in so many ways, yet blessed to be surrounded by a large and loving family.

From nine years of working with hospice patients, I knew what could make her more comfortable.

"We'll go and get some things to help her then come right back," I told her son.

In the car, I told the other nurses, "I wish we had something to help with the secretions. She has so much fluid and she's too weak to cough. In hospice we used Atropine eye drops. We gave them under the tongue and they usually helped."

Lorna had spent the entire last week upstairs in the clinic putting away drugs and other donations. It was an unglamorous job but one that was so needful and she had done it alone and with extreme thoroughness.

"I just saw a bottle of *Atropine Ophthalmic Solution*," she said. "It came in with one of the boxes yesterday and I put it away."

Chills.

"Lorna, God always does this! Whenever I need something, there it is! No matter how rare! I've been at this clinic for fifteen months and not once have we had Atropine eye drops! Until now."

We found the drops, some long-acting Morphine tablets (which we had only a few of, but by faith, the exact number we'd need) a few other supplies, and then we returned.

After we instructed the family how to care for their beloved, I asked if we could pray then nodded to Rosa to begin.

When the seventeen year old girl opened her mouth, she delivered a message of hope with all the authority of Christ Himself.

"Faith is not something you profess once and that's it. It's something you need to grab and hang onto in times like this! Then you'll know that your mother is truly going to a beautiful place, that she's going to be well and at peace, not suffering as she is now!"

She prayed and the Holy Spirit filled the room. We hugged and cried with the various family members and left knowing we had been part of something planned long ago by a sovereign God.

So the story is about Rosa, a student, about Lynda and Lorna, two nurses being obedient to God, Paulina, who hovers between this world and the next, and me, who ponders it all in my heart. However, it's easy to recognize it is first of all a story about Jesus, *"for we are God's workmanship, created in Christ Jesus to do good works, which He prepared in advance for us to do."*

Someday we'll ask Him, "How did you arrange the timing of the eye drops?"

Lorna, Ellie, Rosa, Lynda

February 13, 2009

Glenn Schwartz has a difficult calling. His book, *When Charity Destroys Dignity,* asserts that to simply hand over material gifts to the poor creates dependency. Missionaries and generous Christians the world over recoil at his words. But when he visited us in Baja, his logic sounded familiar to me. From the first time I babysat, my Armenian father encouraged me to work then made me put half my earnings into savings.

"The worst thing you can do to a child is give, give, give without expecting anything from him! Many parents who went through the depression showered the next generation with hand-outs and allowances so their children would not suffer lack. Now they wonder why so many are on welfare, living in debt and feeling entitled!"

In like manner, the greatest Christian thinkers of our time are humbly admitting we need to change the way we do mission. A church, a family, a village, completely dependent on foreign donations will not grow as Christ intended.

A doctor serving in a poor town in South America saw the need for an ambulance. He raised money from his own church in the U.S. and bought one. Then he left for two years. On his return, he inquired what benefit the ambulance had been and the locals told him, "The tires on your vehicle are flat. Please repair them!"

In contrast, when Jesus fed the multitudes, He assessed what resources they had, offered them up to God and they became more than enough. Glenn Schwartz told us of an African church who decided to raise money from within rather than depend on foreign resources. People tithed cows, chickens and grain and raised more than they had dreamed possible. The church grew and multiplied, serving their region with all sorts of ministries.

Glenn reminded us, "It is better to give than to receive.' Do we want to keep that blessing for ourselves?"

So, what exactly did Jesus mean when He said, "Give to the poor?" Well, what did *He* give? First of all, His life. Then teaching, healing, forgiveness, salvation, power, blessings, dignity and hope.

We want to imitate Christ. We are thinking and praying how to put knowledge into practice. Glenn's book says, *"Our world is a very needy place... as Christians we must do what we can. Our challenge is to find a way that preserves dignity and does not create dependency."*

So, will we stop giving out blankets and tarps to those living in cardboard shelters in winter? Surely not. Will we consider in every interaction how we can teach and empower those who are poor that they be made rich? This is our vision.

So we show women in *Jose Dolores* a drama of how a man tires after carrying one man across the river but if he teaches that same man and others how to use the rocks to cross, they can soon all cross by themselves.

And instead of staying with Dirk and Mary, we now send Javier home when he is sick after teaching his family how to care for him.

Betty Swor wants to train a mom whose one year-old son just died to help her care for other sick babies.

In these ways we can give what Jesus did: our lives, our stories, human dignity and divine hope. Please pray for wisdom.

The Poor Bearing Fruit

February 20, 2009

From the standpoint of ministry, the time we spent with nine women in the community of Jose Dolores was pure blessing.

Last week, Angelina, Rosa, and I had arrived at the time we had set with the ladies. The salon was open and several women already inside.

"Wow! They're here waiting for us!" I exclaimed.

A moment later, that excitement plummeted like a wounded duck.

"They're not here for us!" Angelina said. "A government worker is teaching on health and hygiene, and the women chose the time – the same time they told us to come!"

Like rejected suitors, we managed to agree on another date. This time we had no inflated ideas or plans, we simply showed up - the humble stance God looks for. He took control.

When we began with the question, "Do you want to continue with us?" the women answered as one, "Si, hermanas!"

Two volunteers helped us in a short drama depicting holistic health. Senora Lopez had healed from a broken leg but still held vengeance in her heart toward her neighbor whose curse, so she thought, had caused her accident.

"Is she healthy?" I asked.

They divided into small groups to discuss what it means to live in harmony with God, ourselves, others, and the environment. It was while listening to their answers that the Spirit of God moved in me.

Why was I so surprised at the wisdom and depth of their responses? Conviction filled me; after so long, I still thought of the poor as less intelligent! As they spoke, they taught my heart where real riches lie.

"Sometimes people know many things, but if they don't do what they talk about, their knowledge isn't worth anything."

Another said, "We don't have much in material things to give away, but if our neighbor is sad or burdened, we can encourage them, share the word of God."

Leticia, a newcomer, said, "Just because we have silence doesn't mean we have peace. We can be in the house, everything quiet, the kids not making any noise, but if one child is sick or we're angry at someone, we don't have peace. Or there can be lots of noise, the children playing and yelling, very happy and we have peace in our hearts!"

Rosa told me later, "Ellie, I know you wondered why I was taking so long to write down their answers, but I was having trouble not to cry at what they were saying!"

By the time we left, laughter, tears, and sharing thoughts on God and life had broken down walls, empowered the poor, and humbled the rich.

I can not find a word to describe the feeling, but a moment came when I knew I was doing what God had created me for – encouraging, empowering, and bringing freedom to the oppressed, and in the process, being changed myself by the glory of God.

In this place I am learning: much of what we think, is wrong, much of what we do, worthless, and much of what we want, ridiculous. But if we wait upon the Lord, seek first His kingdom and righteousness, all the rest will be given to us.

March 12, 2009

I've had writer's block lately. Plenty has happened; but my mind has been scattered, unable to focus. It's a time of decision for me. The Bible Institute is going on their annual mission trip to Oaxaca, a trip that everyone describes as "grueling." Yet those who have gone tell of incredible spiritual victories attained in communities where darkness and demonic oppression reign. Still, I cringe to think of sleeping communally on a cement floor, spit-showering for a month, and eating foods I usually avoid.

When I voiced my struggle with Enrique, he laughed and hugged me.

"*Mi amada misionera de cinco estrellas! No te preocupes; Dios te cuidará!*"

He was calling me his "beloved five-star missionary" and telling me, "Don't worry; God will take care of you!"

My mind knows he's right. Do I not admire, and *desire*, the great spiritual victories famous missionaries have won? Did Jim Elliott's wife care about her comfort in the jungle as she brought the very people who had murdered her husband to the Lord? Maybe, but doubtful. It is embarrassing to admit that as much as I love the indigenous of Mexico, I still battle with where I sleep, horrid food, and using latrines.

My husband comforts me.

"God knows you're five-star, Ellie. He created you that way! He may take you down one star but never more than you can bear!"

Oddly, while my flesh recoils, my spirit hearkens to the blast of the shofar, calling soldiers to the front lines. I've never understood why men long to go to war but that lust is within me now – to destroy the enemy, to free captives, and bring glory to our King, Who leads us in the battle.

Unfortunately, there is no Marriott on the front line.

March 15, 2009

Now that Victoria has died, she will at last know fullness of life. Many would say the four years she spent in a crippled mind and body was of little value.

"The normal brain has convolutions, like cauliflower; hers is as smooth as a balloon," a neurologist explained. "With so much less surface area, the amount of data her mind can store is minimal, like a computer with insufficient memory. Her prognosis is grave."

Her twenty-one year old mother had brought her to the mission out of desperation. She had two other children to feed and her husband had abandoned them. Betty and Phil accepted her and did what they always do with the babies placed in their home – cared for her twenty-four hours a day with the same love they'd give their own child.

Every time I visited, things seemed worse.

"She's having seizures, long ones, eight to ten times a day."

"There's pus draining out of both ears and the antibiotics aren't helping. Both eardrums are ruptured so the infection can go to her brain."

The worst was the pain.

"She cries for hours and one finger is red because she rubs it against her teeth when she's hurting!"

Her symptoms ran wild - infections, seizures, fever, pain- and our medicines did little.

"She won't eat!"

Betty's voice held fear but I would not give her false consolation.

"She's dying, Betty. The best we can do is make her comfortable."

Dominga, Victoria's mother gave us permission to start using codeine for the pain. She understood her daughter was dying.

"Whatever you think best, sisters," she replied with the blanket acceptance that life is hard.

That was three weeks ago. Since then we adjusted and readjusted anticonvulsants, antibiotics, codeine and Tylenol while Betty cared for her motionless body with tenderness. Saturday evening she called me. Rushing over, I found the child feverish with labored gurgling respirations. In her crib were five thermometers.

"What's all this?" I asked.

"The first one read 107 degrees," explained Betty. "Phil and I didn't believe it so we tried all these."

We sponged her with tepid water, put ice packs on her groins, and administered drops to dry up the phlegm. Slowly her body cooled and her breathing eased. No pain, no convulsions, she was finally at peace. Holiness surrounded her and soothed us. I rested one of her calves in my palm. There was no muscle tone in this leg that had never walked. Yet she had a small scar on her knee. Fixated on this pale crescent shape blemish, I wondered how it had occurred. I remembered falling off my bike as a child and running home to show the cut to my mother who washed it and dried my tears. The scar it left looked like Victoria's so I began to imagine her riding a bike or playing hide-and-seek with her siblings.

People began to visit – Dirk, Dana, Mario, Jorge. Sometime during their visit, each one touched her, stroking her arm, face, or chest. They may have believed they were doing it to comfort her but she had comfort we could only long for!

Victoria, serene and innocent, was on her way to Jesus. Shrouded in beauty and mystery, our souls were drawn to her as a moth to light. We could not touch what we hungered for, only the soft silkiness of her skin, yet it was enough.

She died in the morning, in a comfortable crib, her upper body supported on a pillow.

"If only for this life we have hope in Christ, we are to be pitied more than all men." (1 Corinth. 15:19)

There was no beauty or purpose to Victoria's life if not divine. In the afternoon, Enrique led the congregation in worship. We sang these words, "here we are, before your throne." With all my effort I sang to please God. But suddenly I pictured Victoria face-to-face with Jesus and entered into true worship, imagining her joy made full by His glory.

"For you died, and your life is now hidden with Christ in God. When Christ, Who is your life, appears, then you also will appear with Him in glory."
(Col. 3:3-4)

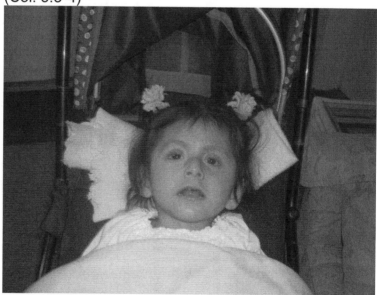

Victoria

March 25, 2009
"Blessed are the poor!"

Although it was Jesus Himself Who said this, how many of us truly believe it? Sure, we may accept it in some unexamined way as we sip tea on our patio. But can we look into the face of suffering that poverty causes and echo Christ's assessment, "Blessed are the poor?"

An indigenous woman came to the clinic last week looking for Dr. Avitia. A medical doctor as well as a pastor, Ramón Avitia has the heart of both. The woman told us her grandson had died on Sunday. Her hands moved feverishly, like wringing an invisible washcloth over and over.

"He's in the casket and we were going to bury him this afternoon! But we think he may be still alive! One woman thought she felt his heart beat, very weakly, but...Please, doctor, come and check him!"

Other family members were with her and we followed their car to the two-room house. Cristofer, twelve months old, laid in an open white casket, was gorgeous. The second son of a teenage couple, indeed, he seemed merely asleep. His skin was still pink and in repose, super-long eyelashes gave his face a feminine touch. Otherwise he was all boy, and his three-piece white suit felt wrong. He should have been in toddler's jeans and a soiled sweatshirt proudly taking wobbly first steps.

But he was dead. As gently as possible the doctor confirmed it to the breathless family. As if he had died a second time, they cried and let go of hope.

Had I turned to the young couple and spoke Jesus' words, "Blessed are you who are poor, who weep now, who mourn," it would have been heartless. Only in time could it become clear that in their great lack – of a son, of money, of understanding – could they arrive at a place of no false hope, no enticements of the world to hold onto.

"Your son is with Jesus," the pastor said. "If you want to go where he is, be with him one day forever, you need to follow Jesus."

The father answered in a soft firm voice.

"My wife has already accepted Christ into her heart. Today I want to, also."

Ramón, the pastor, led him in a prayer to become a Christian then asked God to comfort and bless the whole family.

Three people came to Christ this week through the clinic; all, poor, and all ultimately blessed. Thomas Merton wrote, "Poverty is the door to freedom...finding nothing in ourselves (or this life) that is a source of hope... we go out of ourselves and rest in Him in Whom alone is our hope."

These three precious new believers can pray now as Merton did: "My Lord, I have no hope but in Your Cross. Why should I cherish in my heart a hope that devours me – the hope for perfect happiness in this life – when such hope, doomed to frustration, is nothing but despair? My hope is in what the eye has never seen."

Blessed are the poor, then, whose faith does not depend on material comforts, health, or circumstances. How many rich people's faith waxes and wanes with the "felt" blessings of God? Take them away - will faith remain? I am speaking to myself.

"God has chosen those who are poor in the eyes of the world to be rich in faith," James tells us, *"and to inherit the kingdom He promised those who love Him."*

God is omniscient. If He says, *"Blessed are the poor!"* then it is true.

April 22, 2009

Everything about Culiacán, Sinaloa is very. The ranches, very large; the ranch-owners, very rich; the climate, very hot, and the farmworkers, very poor, very oppressed, and very open to the gospel.

Huge camps house migrant workers in scenes reminiscent of Nazi Germany. People robbed of their dignity and hope co-existing in long rows of tin housing, never making enough money to escape.

We had heard many reports from teams that had visited earlier. As our bus rumbled down the highway from the airport, what grabbed our attention were giant silos towering over mile-long cornfields. We barely noticed the migrant camps. Although much larger than the missile-like storehouses of grain, the camps sprawled out low to the ground and colorless. Nothing rose up to make a statement. They had been planned to squash upward designs.

In Baja the wealthy are few, so the disparity between rich and poor is hidden.

Not so in Culiacán. Downtown, a boulevard of car dealerships offer high-status cars for sale. In communion with the ranchers, farm equipment and pesticide companies share the wealth of the industry. While men negotiate and earn fortunes, their beautiful wives stroll a super-mall in tight clothes and high heels buying up the latest fashions.

"Picture Culiacán like Texas," Enrique, my dear Mexican husband, described to me. "Wealthy ranchers who speak with a drawl and exaggerate everything to the biggest and the best! And don't forget it is also known as *"la cuna de los narcotraficantes"* nursery of drug traffickers. The first international cartel started here."

Truly, the rich live off the stolen lives of the poor. Our tomatoes, corn, strawberries are cheap because many people, whom God fashioned and loves, work for criminally-low wages and have no voice.

Shopping was a vice I struggled with before living on the reduced income of a missionary. It was a pleasant waste of time for me to browse a mall and buy clothes that I liked but didn't need. The lavish mall in downtown Culiacán brought the seduction of advertising to a fine art. Mannequins in darling dresses called me over like girlfriends and each store seemed more colorful than the last. But it was too soon after our visit to a camp of two thousand inhabitants. Every price tag made me calculate how many people could be fed. The excess of jewelry, the absolute glut of every material item made me marvel at the patience of our Lord. If it sickened me, a shopper, what sadness did our heavenly Father feel to see injustice, greed, and lack of compassion for the oppressed? Fortunately, most of them could not afford the bus fare to see this unimaginable place.

Please pray for an upheaval of the whole system of ranching, that the workers would receive decent wages, healthcare benefits, and education for their children. And the next time you head off to the mall, please buy one less item and send what you save to the poor. The blessing is guaranteed or your money back!

Workers' Housing

April 30, 2009

If the children are the heart of the orphanage, Javier is the pulse, circulating joy throughout the mission. His body is skeletal, his legs too weak to stand on. Lung infections plague him and at fourteen, he suffers the indignity of having to be either pushed in a wheelchair or carried wherever he goes.

"He can not learn to count to three!" Mary Kos told me recently. "Yet he remembers the names of visitors who worked with him a year ago!"

Muscular Dystrophy has stolen the life out of his body but is unable to defeat Javier's spirit, which finds strength in the Lord and people. When the day home closed for health risks concerning the swine flu, Javier was sad. Then a "Children's Day" event in which my clown, Luci, was scheduled to perform at his house, was also postponed. For this extroverted child, nothing was worse than to be away from his friends. No surprise, then, that his family called to report him ill.

"A fever, cough, vomiting and stomach pain," Mary told me the symptoms. "This is the third time he's gotten sick when we closed the school."

"Sure! I hate to think of him in that wheel chair all day with nothing to do, missing everyone. The discouragement lowers his immune system and with no reserves - boom! he's sick!."

Because of the danger of swine flu, we agreed it would place the orphanage at risk if we visited him at home.

"Let's call him!" I suggested as an alternative.

We called his aunt who held the phone to his ear.

"Hola, Ellie."

His voice was flat and I was desperate to cheer him.

"I miss you! Papa Cate and Mary miss you, too! We don't want you to be sad, so we're going to keep calling you all weekend! Okay?"

"Our calls will be his antibiotic," I told Mary.

Next we made a street call.

"We can't enter the house," I explained to his Aunt Victoria. "But this is what we can do…"

Javier loves Enrique's worship. So we planned a short concert for him and for his brother, Feliciano. We parked along the dirt road in front of their house. The family brought the boys out in their wheelchairs. Then Enrique started to play his guitar and sing praise songs the boys knew, the whole family joining the celebration. Javier looked radiant.

"He seems better!" I commented to Maria, his grandmother.

"He started to improve right after the first time you called! His fever came down and he stopped vomiting. He was so excited to talk to you, and then Dirk called and now, Enrique's music - you people healed him!"

My heart rejoiced in the sweetness of our God! The Lord is the One Who healed him, of course, but He used our phone calls and music to do it. Javier showed us, in a concrete manner, that love and joy heal.

"A cheerful heart is good medicine, but a crushed spirit dries up the bones." (Prov. 17:22)

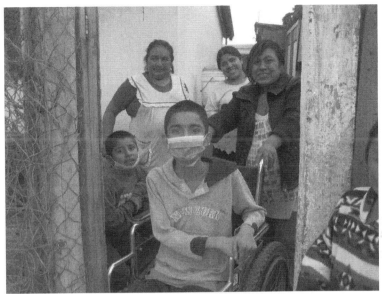
Javier and Family

My husband, the Wandering Minstrel

May 8, 2009

Like his mother, Reynaldo was born with six fingers on each hand. Three were fused together so he could not grasp or hold things. Marta had come to the clinic a long time ago seeking intervention, not for herself, but for her son. We kept her contact information and three weeks ago, Dr. Justin Sherfey, an orthopedic surgeon, and a group of podiatry students visited the mission. We called Marta and the doctor examined her two-year old's hands.

"One has too many nerves and bones. I can't do that here," said Justin. "but we can amputate the sixth digit on the right hand because it only contains cartilage, and we can separate the fingers."

Great news! The surgery on Friday went smoothly, but Saturday, mom came back worried. Reynaldo had pulled off the dressing and the dry drainage from the wounds had fused the fingers together again. Ciry, a full-time nurse, and Dirk soaked and scrubbed gently until they were loose again. It was as painful as it sounds, but successful.

We did dressing changes every two days, and then the day came to remove the sutures. It was yet another painful procedure for this darling brave boy, who cried at the worst parts but still kissed me goodbye at the end.

The wounds healed to the point where we began to move his fingers slightly - forward, back, apart, and into a curl.

"Do this with him at home!" I told Marta. "Stop if it hurts, but we don't want them to get stiff."

The last visit yesterday, was full of victories. Reynaldo didn't cry when he saw me. He loved the fluffy white bunny I gave him and best of all,

"He's moving the fingers by himself!" mom announced.

The little guy must have wondered why fanning his fingers made four women cry. The whole clinic staff: Nora, Angelina, Ciry, and I took turns hugging him and Marta.

Justin Sherfey, in one day, changed Reynaldo's life forever. You don't have to be a surgeon to do this. Visitors do it all the time, sharing love, talents, time, and hearts with God's most precious commodity: children.

June 7, 2009

A writer has the burden of choosing which story gets told while letting others go silent. Our trip to Oaxaca deserves a book to applaud each life God touched, each spiritual victory He achieved. One night in Juxtlahuaca, (don't even try to pronounce it!) it came to me that the story that includes every other is that of the Holy Spirit! The wonderful unity of our team, even when exhausted after long days of clinic, the miraculous freedom inside a maximum security section of a Oaxacan prison, the joy shared with children in mountain villages – each was a chapter of the amazing story of our amazing God!

I felt a correct sense of humility on this trip, a deep knowledge that every good thing accomplished had been done by God. When Pastor Bill Dwyer preached one night at a pastors' conference, he spoke a truth worth remembering.

"God was concerned about Oaxaca before we were born! He was concerned about the Jewish people enslaved in Egypt before Moses was born. The man who led the Jews through the desert was, like us, simply a part of God's toolbox!"

Daniel, a young man in prison, asked, "Where was God when my mother abandoned me at birth? When I was raped at age seven by someone who called himself a Christian, when I was addicted to heroin as a teen?"

Tough questions, no simple answers. Yet by faith we maintained the certainty that God had always been concerned about this abused child and had a masterful plan for Daniel's salvation, healing, joy, and victory. Members of our team listening to his pain, loving, counseling and praying for him was part of that plan. He lost the fear and mistrust of Christians caused by past hurts. He welcomed a sense of peace, friendship of other believers, and freedom inside a prison that no longer held his soul.

The Holy Spirit gave me a unique anointing as I taught and played with fifty children in the village of Santa Cecelia Jalieza. We used green glitter to learn how germs are passed and it was much harder to wash off than microbes.

"What's on your face, Ellie?" team members asked.

One tried to rub the green sparkles off my face; another wet a paper towel and tried to wash them away, but I delighted in the laughter it caused the children. We ran around blowing bubbles, then practiced brushing our teeth and washing our hands, and they learned a few words in English.

At the end of the day, kids surrounded me, asking, "When are you coming back?"

It cost me a lot to leave them; we had become one by the Spirit of God in play.

I answered, "Maybe next year," and when they showed disappointment, I urged them, "Seek God and He'll bless your lives!"

Doctors, dentists, nurses and optometrists used their trade to reach the hearts of the poor and they did it with great love, but the most dramatic healings came through prayer and the sharing of the word of God. That's why this narrative is about the third person of the Trinity. He is the life, author, and main character of every tale worth telling.

June 12, 2009

During a medical outreach in a mountain village, a woman, Maguera, asked if we could visit her aged mother.

"She had a stroke and has trouble speaking. Also, she sleeps a lot."

We had worked all day and now it was dark. Thunder and lightning warned of an approaching Oaxacan downpour. The patient was ninety-six years old, could still swallow and move all her extremities. I wanted to say, "Praise God!" but the daughter looked so concerned.

Roberto, our team leader, was a godly man, full of life and prayer.

"I found someone to drive us to where the road ends, but he says the house is in a gulley and we'll have to walk from there."

Rain spattered the windshield and our headlights illuminated one sharp turn after another through jungle terrain. When it seemed like we were truly nowhere, he pulled over and shut off the engine.

"It's down there" he said, pointing.

If a huge lightning bolt hadn't lit up the landscape, we'd never have seen the trail. One of the daughters came up to lead us with a flashlight. The night was ink black; all we could see were our feet, and some mud and rocks beneath them.

"Whoa!"

A huge bolt of lightning flashed in the sky ahead and for one moment, night turned into day.

"I feel more like Kathleen Turner and Indiana Jones than missionaries on a house call!" I told Roberto.

The flash showed us the sky and clouds, silhouetted the tops of pine trees and illuminated our steep descent. Shortly we made it to the bottom where Maguera led us into the second of two rooms inside a cement house. Another daughter leaned over a mound of blankets on the only bed and called to her mom.

As if dust were reforming into life, the ancient Indian woman sat up. Her hair was white and braided, her skin told of years in the sun. When she spoke, the words were as garbled as the bedding.

"I can't talk!" we made out.

"I would love to know what you have to say," I answered.

Ninety-six years in these mountains and her wisdom was locked inside.

"Keep trying!" I encouraged Maria, the elder, and her three daughters. "Especially practice the sounds that are hard! And be sure she swallows whatever you feed her or she could choke."

I started to teach them basic nursing skills, but the rain turned torrential. The lights went out and the roaring of hard rain on a tin roof drowned out speech. We stood in the blackness, silent and waiting. The lights came on and went off twice more before we were ready to leave. As always when a family cares for a loved one, the burden fell back on them, but also the blessing.

I encouraged them with the truth.

"You're doing a great job! This is a very special time and your mom could not be more blessed than to be at home with three caring daughters!"

"Why not stay and have a cup of tea, wait for the rain to stop?" Maguera offered.

Sounded like a great idea to me but Roberto thought of the team.

"We have to get back," he said.

The downpour had not let up and the path up to the truck had turned to mud in the storm. We stood under an overhang on the cement patio. Looking around, somewhat desperate, I noticed a flowery plastic tablecloth on a wooden table.

"Can we use that?" I blurted out.

"Sure!"

Maguera's husband handed it to me and I held it over my head and body. We found another one on the inside table and Roberto used it to cover himself. As hard as we tried, we couldn't convince the humble sturdy Maguera to use protection. She led us into the rain wearing a simple fleece jacket while Roberto and I traipsed into the deluge looking like weird animals in a children's pageant.

The scene struck me as hilarious and I began to sing. I made up my own words to the tune of a praise song, mixing English with Spanish and making Roberto laugh.

"La lluvia (rain) de Dios es maravillosa, the lluvia de Dios es maravillosa, la lluvia de Dios es maravillosa, tan grande is the rain of God!"

This was the visit I had judged "unnecessary." Yet by going, I got to "act" in an adventure written and directed by the Lord. I can hardly wait for the sequels!

June 13 2009

"Do you know the laws of the heavens? Can you set up God's dominion over the earth?"

God was asking Job if he considered himself of equal intelligence with Him. One of those questions your father asks when you've questioned his authority, like "Who pays the rent around here?"

To his credit, Job repented immediately of any mistrust when the Lord appeared. He groveled.

"Surely I spoke of things I did not understand, things too wonderful for me to know."

Still, the Lord praised Job because even though he'd whined a little, his faith never put demands on God.

"Though He slay me, yet will I will trust in Him!"

So many of us refuse to trust God unless He meets our expectations.

"I'm HIV positive," Edgar told us from inside a Oaxacan prison, "and starting to be sick all the time! People talk to me about God and I listen, but I keep praying for Him to heal me and He hasn't!"

In the mountains, thirteen year-old Magele told me she'd survived her mother's attempt to abort her.

"She took herbs to stop the pregnancy because it was not by her husband, but I was born anyway. Later she went to live with my father but rejected all her children."

She was crying so hard it was difficult to understand her words.

"I heard about Jesus and converted. Every day I pray for my mother to come back to us. I talk to her about God but she doesn't want to hear anything about that!"

Her tears fell freely; she didn't wipe them away. I was drowning in her grief until God revealed His heart and gave me these words.

"You've been greatly wounded, Magele, but you are precious to God. He entered your mother's body before you were even born to save you! He has a plan for your life! Come close to Him for the healing you need, for the love of a mother and of a father that you never received. Don't make reconciliation with your mother the most important thing! Let God be God of all your life! He'll heal you and love you!"

She clung to me a long time, sobbing. Not wanting her to feel the slightest reenactment of her mother's rejection, I would not end the embrace. I would have stayed forever in that mountaintop church if she hadn't finally let me go.

Later, I attended a three-language church service. Pastor Bill taught, "We are very different, but in Christ, we are one." The congregation included missionaries from Baja, Oaxaca, and Los Angeles, and Mixtecan Indians.

I smiled at a tiny, grey-haired Triqui woman who wore a brightly-colored woven sack-dress. How many times I'd seen that dress and thought *how beautiful the embroidery and ribbons!* Only on this trip did I learn it was the equivalent of the Moslem "burka," used to show that the woman belongs to someone, not as a treasured wife but as a possession. If this woman were now a Christian, why didn't she live in freedom, and abandon the demeaning dress?

When Bill talked about David, the shepherd boy, trusting God, new awareness came to me. What I wanted for the woman in the Oaxacan burka may not happen, as Edgar may not be healed of AIDS nor Magele's mother become the local PTA president.

"But if we trust God," Bill said, "He'll bless our lives."

The grey-haired woman may die working in some field, but she'll die at peace with God and go immediately into the same Holy Presence as the wealthiest believer on earth.

More and more I realize that some of my desires may be inappropriate, even for my own life. Sometimes I have the good sense to surrender my wishes and ask only that God's will to be done. When my will merges with His, I am swallowed up in loveliness.

Ellie and Magele

June 27, 2009

A week before leaving for Oaxaca, in a Tijuana church, my husband had led worship, his rich voice and sincere passion ushering in the presence of God. The Pastor, another Enrique, made a fervent cry for the people of God to seek Him more fully. I had been one of several kneeling on the floor, my heart yearning to do more for Him.

"Speak about abuse!" I distinctly heard Him say.

However, when we arrived in Oaxaca, local pastors and missionaries cautioned me, "You have to be careful, Ellie! Talking on that subject here can be dangerous for you and the other women!"

So I waited, but with expectation that the Lord would open a door. Each time our medical team did an outreach, I taught those waiting to be seen: handwashing, dental care, the importance of breastfeeding and of forgiveness - and each time the men of the village stood by, stern-faced and observant. I dared not teach what I most wanted.

"Lord, there's only one more day!"

Our last clinic was in La Jolla Putla, a mountain village. It was a beautiful setting, on the patio of a light-blue church in a valley sixty-three steps below the street. We were high in the mountains but the peaks rose higher still, emerald and thick with trees. The hot humid air was as stifling as the culture.

"What is your community's worst health problem?" I asked.

Two Indian women sat side-by-side embroidering hand towels.

"Alcoholism!" said one. "Many people here drink and use drugs."

Great, I thought, can't we start with an easier topic? Colds, high blood pressure, for which there are simple facts?

"Addictions affect a lot more people than those who are using, don't they?" I asked.

What followed was more of a sharing than a teaching, but the poor have a deep need to be heard. I would not insult them with simple answers.

We moved on to my favorite part of the Health Education Program For Developing Countries.

"The most important knowledge we have that affects health is that God loves each of us and we also should love one another. Believing and acting upon this knowledge alone would prevent much of our heart disease, stomach problems, cancers, mental health problems, headaches, high blood pressure, not to mention war and terrorism!"

The Holy Spirit whispered, "Now!"

I looked at my immediate audience and saw it was all women except a harmless-looking old blind man.

"And abuse!" I quickly added. "Many people abuse their spouse or children, not just here in Oaxaca, but around the world! They hit them and yell at them, control them through fear, disrespect, and isolation."

Oaxacan women avoid your eyes unless they know you. Their downward and sideways glances made me feel like I were selling something they didn't want. I forged ahead.

"This is not what God intended for matrimony! The Bible says, *'a husband should love his wife!'* So, what is love? 1st Corinthians 13 says, *'love is patient, love is kind, love does not anger easily.'* Is your husband patient with you? Is he kind? Does he anger easily? None of us is perfect, but if you are constantly afraid, if you are not free to be the person God created you to be, that's not love!"

Now I had their attention.

"I can't tell you to leave your marriage. Most of you have children, no money, nowhere to go. However, if you feel unsafe, you should find shelter, perhaps with the pastor here or a relative! Apart from that, know that God cares about you! Come to Him! We can pray with you today. Then find two other Christian women to meet with and pray regularly for your families! God can change a man's heart. He's your Father and He'll do a great work if you ask Him!"

Now their eyes met mine. They lifted up their heads; some nodded. One let out an emphatic, "Si, hermana!"

In that moment came strength and victory. We had dragged abuse into the Light, robbing its authority. Education and the Word of God bestowed power, hope and, yes, even freedom, to sisters with the same needs as I.

"But what did you accomplish?" you might ask.

"The will of God," my response.

Now they have understanding, about which the Bible promises:

" whoever finds me (wisdom) finds life and receives favor from the Lord." (Prov. 8:35)

Life and favor from the Lord – what more can I desire for my oppressed sisters?

Tales of A Five-Star Missionary

July 17, 2009

Once upon a time Christian missionaries believed that if we gave medicines to poor people, they would be healed, see Jesus in our actions, and receive salvation. The best Christian medical minds now know this rarely happens. What is much more likely is that poor people come to believe that doctors from the United States or other developed countries have powerful medicines that cure every health problem. If the missionaries run a healthcare facility, people come in for every cough and cold or minor aches and pains. They are disappointed if they don't walk away with at least three drugs.

Three-quarters of the ailments for which people come to our clinic in Baja are things for which, otherwise, they would not seek treatment, and which their immune systems could easily heal. But a free clinic giving out free meds encourages them to seek aggressive care for a minor cough that began "last night." We have made them dependent - on us and on medications.

"The truth is that not a single cough or cold remedy has been proven effective in curing colds or even reducing complications. But families all over the world go hungry so they can afford to buy these medicines."

This information comes from the "Health Education Program For Developing Countries." (hepfdc.org) In simple language with color illustrations, it contains the very best knowledge available from the World Health Organization and other world health expert agencies. I use it to explain that cough and cold remedies are ineffective and have dangerous side effects, especially for children.

"What has been proven effective for coughs and colds is to drink lots of liquids, take Vitamin C in natural forms, breast feed babies, rest, give lots of TLC and pray."

To encourage poor Indian mothers to spend loving time with their children may be the start of new behavior. Their culture does not prioritize nurturing of the young. One million babies die each year from infections which could have been prevented had they been breast-fed.

It takes a lot more time to teach than to hand out drugs. First, you have to listen with compassion and gain trust. Then you must explain in love why you are not giving an antibiotic for a virus nor any of the cold treatments the patient knows we Americans have.

Yesterday, a visiting nurse was considering giving a liquid cough medicine she found on the shelf. I stopped her and we gave the mother teaching and expert advice instead. Later I researched the two medicines the suspension contained.

"Carbetapentane tannate" is a decongestant/antihistamine which "acts on the brain to decrease the urge to cough and helps relieve stuffy nose and itchy watery eyes, nose and throat." The side effects are: "drowsiness, dizziness, flushing, headache, nausea, nervousness, blurred vision, dry mouth/nose/throat, mood changes, hallucinations, tremors, trouble urinating, weakness, fast/slow/irregular heartbeat, seizure."

Who the heck would give this to their child? The instructions read: "Ask your doctor about other ways to relieve cough and cold symptoms (like saline nose drops, humidifier.) They suggest you "drink plenty of fluids when you use the med" and tell you "the fluid will help loosen the mucus in your lungs."

However, the warning on the second ingredient in the liquid, "Chlorpheniramine tannate," reads: Chlorpheniramine can dry up and thicken mucus in your lungs, making it more difficult to breathe and clear your lungs."

So you need to drink *more* liquids to try to undue the harmful effects of the medicine! And why would anyone with a respiratory infection take a drug which "can dry up and thicken mucus in your lungs, making it more difficult to breathe and clear your lungs?"

The cough suppressant that "decreases the urge to cough" can block the body's design to clear the lungs of mucus and allow the phlegm to stagnate, grow bacteria and causing pneumonia.

As a missionary I want to serve the poor in "the most excellent way." To teach them information from world health experts, to withhold medicines which have no proven benefits and create lots of harm, to listen and to pray – this, to me, is love. I may need to talk myself blue in the face, repeating the same thing over and over to every impoverished mom in the valley, but I am in good company. Jesus taught. He did no harm - the physician's oath - and He showed people how to change their lives for the better. Restored to dignity and health, people believed and gave praise to God.

."*Jesus went throughout Galilee, teaching in their synagogues, preaching the good news of the kingdom, and healing every disease and sickness among the people.*"

(Matt. 4:23)

Using the Health Education Program For Developing Countries

August 30, 2009

A frequent prayer of mine is, "Lord, let me see enough fruit to be encouraged but not enough that I may get proud!"

Hopefully, He's hiding some, because I sure don't see enough to be proud.

Universidad Autónoma de Baja California or "UABC" is a Mexican university with a branch in Ensenada. This week was the second time they sent a large group of medical students to work in our clinic. Greeting the fifth-semester students, I thought about how, in my career as a nurse, new doctors started out older than I, then became my peers, and now they looked like children! For three days these bright eager youngsters attended our mission staff as well as the local population.

First, though, I gathered them for a welcome speech and educational presentation stressing three points:

1. The importance of listening. "Listen to the patient's heart! Often, he or she has a much deeper need than what they verbalize. God made us body, mind and soul, and one affects the others. We must treat the whole person!"
2. "Do No Harm! Teach more, prescribe less!" I told them adverse drug effects are now the fourth leading cause of death (according to World Health Org.) and there's higher risk when doctors come in short-term with language and cultural barriers." Even though these students were Mexican, most of our patients were Indian and, therefore, a different culture. Specifically, I told about the dangers of Ibuprofen and other anti-inflammatories, the worthlessness of cough and cold remedies, and that Nimesulide, commonly used in Mexico, had been banned in twenty other countries and should not be used.

3. The Placebo Effect. "Research now shows that what we believe will work to heal us has a sixty-percent better chance of doing so! Jesus said, 'Your faith has healed you!' and science is now proving He was right! You, as doctors, have power to affect what people put their faith in – God and self-healing or drugs!"

I gave them permission not to prescribe drugs to every patient and requested they do daily health education presentations. It seemed to have gone well, but sitting in on a few consultations, I was appalled at how many meds they prescribed, especially unnecessary injections! As for teaching, it took four requests to the doctor in charge before they complied.

"We will!"

"It's too crowded!"

"It's too noisy!" she told me at different times.

Finally we put up a tarp outside for shade and herded patients to that area. I offered a microphone system to the student assigned to teach. With that, I got one token lesson on "Obesity."

Sometimes I feel like an accomplice for being present when people are guided toward drugs rather than prevention and natural means of healing. Yet, God tells me to stay and keep trying. Maybe one of these bright young doctors will hear, will consider deeply what it means to "do no harm." If one poor Indian mom believes that breastfeeding and love can help her baby more than cough syrup, that's enough to keep me going.

"Let us not become weary in doing good, for at the proper time we will reap a harvest if we do not give up."

(Gal. 6:9)

UABC Students

September 23 2009

The infant girls were a female Jacob and Esau, together in the womb and battling for the blessing from the day they were born. Denia, the firstborn, was red-skinned and indifferent, lounging in her mother's arms. Dania, the younger, looked like a caffeinated hatchling – with beady, alert eyes and not wasting precious time asleep.

When mom and the seven-year old big sister carried them into the clinic, they became the main event. We stopped everything to ooh and aah, cuddle and weigh them, and interview the mom.

"Are you breastfeeding them?" I asked.

"I'm trying," she responded. "Dania wants to nurse all the time so I'm having to give Denia the bottle."

No wonder the little squirt looked so healthy; she was hogging all the food! I took pity on little Esau-ette, who was getting robbed of the blessing. Mom listened while I encouraged her to persevere because breast milk was crucial for good health and development (especially for this weakling, I didn't add.)

"I'll gather information on breastfeeding twins. Come back in a few days, okay?"

La Leche League, the Health Ed Program, and Betty Swor, who cares for our sick babies, gave me lots of practical and expert advice. The best tip was the most obvious: "Let the one who eats less, eat first! The stronger one can eat second and stimulate the breast to make more!"

The bottom line is what Jacob didn't learn till much later in his life – with God, there is always enough for everyone, whether it's milk or blessing. So let the strong help the weak; the rich help the poor, and everyone will see the glory of God!

Denia and Dania

October 2, 2009

Sandra Cordoba loves to worship! This morning, her voice cut through all the others, its intensity, the fruit of her intimacy with the Lord. The song carried me into His presence, as well, but the source of such a heartfelt song drew me to wonder. She was deep in private adoration, still, I had to look at her. A gorgeous young woman, she has rich brown hair and dark almond-shaped eyes which often express what her mouth can not. Her head leaned slightly down and to the right; arms extended stiffly out in front. By the furrowed brow and pouting lips, one may have thought she was in pain, but I knew it was pure passion.

"the Spirit Himself intercedes for us with groans that words cannot express." (Romans 8:26)

To the untuned ear, Sandra's song sounded like plaintive moaning, but for those who listened deeper, it was prayer, love, and longing.

"Gracias, Cristo!" we sang over and over.

Sandra's gratefulness to God is profound. Yet she's confined to a wheelchair by Cerebral Palsy and dependent on others for all her care. Few people at the mission understand her garbled speech, so, many, as I did at first, assume she is mentally handicapped. The truth is she's brighter than most!

Two years ago, after I'd become accustomed to walking by her or throwing her a quick smile, she gave her testimony in sala. A friend had taken the time to listen and write it all down. Standing beside her, she read us the story of Sandra's life: the complications at her birth, her father's faithful care, and her strong dependence on Jesus Christ. The fact that struck me speechless was how vastly I had underestimated her. Here was an intelligent woman with a great sense of humor, knowledge of two languages, the ability to write music, and an absolute passion for the Lord and His people!

"Lord, I want more of you! Lord, I want more of you! I want to feel you in me all of my days!"

Sandra wrote these lyrics and we sang them with her in sala. Respect for the woman made me want to run over and bow to her, like the queen she is. What she desires most, is not a healthy body or clear speech, but ever-increasing intimacy with her Savior!

Sandra and I are now friends. It takes effort to listen to her brand of speech and understand, but in doing so, I grasp her true beauty and relish her constant love and joy.

Thank-you, God, for using her to remind me - You hide Your greatest treasures to be found by those who really seek them!

"Show me your face, let me hear your voice; for your voice is sweet, and your face is lovely."
(Song of Solomon 2:14)

Sandra Cordoba

October 20, 2009
"One man's pleasure is another man's poison."
Whoever said this must not have believed in absolutes. Seems to me arsenic is arsenic, whether you like the taste or hate it. And sugar, no matter if ninety-nine percent of us love it and are addicts, is still poison for our bodies.

"What does sugar have to do with a missionary's life?" you might ask.

It's because poor mothers, just like rich ones, desire to give treats to their children. Candy is cheap, so families whose diet consists of tortillas and beans, and whose kids have never tasted an orange, still manage to overdose their kids on sugar. Filthy adorable toddlers come in the clinic with colds, diarrhea, even pneumonia, sucking on lollipops. Many children have blackened rotten teeth and their tongues are blue, green, or purple from some dyed sugary "treat."

It's a desperate situation, because of which God has called me to teach parents, children, everyone, the truth: the effects of sugar on our health is anything but sweet! Obesity is right behind smoking as the most common cause of preventable diseases and death worldwide. Diabetes and cancer are striking the young and sugar is directly linked to both.

In Jose Dolores, my friend Kathy and I taught an interactive class on the harmful effects of sugar.

"Azúcares, glucosa, dextrosa, jarabe de maíz, fructosa."

The women read the many names for sugar from the ingredients listed on their children's favorite snacks.

"Sugar can cause anxiety, high blood pressure, diabetes, cancer, irritability, mood swings, depression, attention deficit and many other chronic illnesses."

The moms listened. One even nudged her five year-old daughter and told her, "Listen!"

"How much sugar do we eat?" I asked them. "Well, let's see! One hundred years ago, the average person ate five pounds a year."

I held up a two kilogram bag to show them how much 4.4 pounds was. They lifted eyebrows and said, *"Es mucho!"* ("That's a lot!")

"We eat a lot more now!" I continued. "Today the average person, in one form or another, often without realizing, eats two to three pounds of sugar per week!

I showed them a one-kilogram or 2.2 pound bag. Then, so they would grasp that this only represented one week, compared to a year, we carried in fifty-two one-kilogram bags of sand from our truck. Some of the children helped, making several trips back and forth from the classroom.

"Twenty-six! That's only June!" I shouted, heading out for more.

Finally we had all fifty-two lined up on the cement floor. Both the children and their mothers expressed astonishment over the quantity.

It's a strange calling – to take candy away from Mexican children. But if God can use me to put fruits and vegetables into the cavity-filled mouths of these obese, undernourished children, I will be as blessed as they.

Lots of Sugar!

October 28, 2009

New England at the peak of autumn is a mood-altering display of God's joy. Fall's rainbow turns the woods brilliant: red, yellow and orange-leafed trees, and their upside-down reflections in lakes and ponds double the beauty.

Halloween misses the point, celebrating darkness instead of light and fear instead of joy. My mother, a member of the Silver Newtones, a choral group for seniors, invited me to their holiday show at the Mount Pleasant Skilled Nursing Facility in Boston.

The parlor was filled with aged residents of the home, some whose minds had wandered far, others frail only in body. "Dem Bones" started the show, a song created from the book of Ezequiel when God brought life to dry bones. The use of this Christian song to stir up pagan celebration disturbed me. Then Mom performed the song "Memories" as a solo. Her voice was still clear and lovely but I longed to hear the traditional worship she had sung for years in church – "Panis Angelicus," "The Holy City," "Ave Maria." Now, dressed like a cat, she sang in a group which did not allow the name of Jesus. Although the more infirm residents seemed unaware of the music, I wished for something more edifying.

"Oh, that they would worship You, Lord!" I prayed.

"Now we'll take a peek into what the Devil does in his leisure time!"

Joan, the choral director, introduced the song, "Devil's Ball" in this manner and I sank into a leaden place, unable to feel anything but a desperate burden for these who would sing so lightly about hell.

When one man shouted with a bass voice, "And a lot of my friends were there!" I reached a breaking point. My choices were clear: to run out of the room in tears or to pray with the strength of a warrior.

"Lord, forgive them, they know not what they say! Jesus, overcome this darkness with Your light! Fill their hearts with Your presence!"

Next, Shirley Jackson came up, an old black woman with a gospel style, She steered us away from ghosts and goblins and managed to end her set with a rousing chorus of "Amen!" Then she handed the mike to Josefa, a ninety-six year old whose hair was as pure white as her cleansed-by-Jesus soul.

"She doesn't speak English!" someone yelled.

"No matter," Shirley answered.

Josefa stood in front of the Halloween chorus and began to worship the Lord in her native Spanish. Maybe I was the only one in this Irish Catholic nursing home who understood her words, but everyone knew she was praising God.

"You are king of heaven and earth, the great Jehovah! Shine your light here, Lord, shine Your light for all to see!"

In that moment, a Costa Rican grandma, repulsed by the idolatry around her, had taken control. This ancient Christian sister chased away my despair and the joy of the Lord took its place.

"You have been a great blessing to me!" I told her later. "I wanted God to take control, to bring His light – and through you, it happened!"

"I'm ninety-six years old," she said, "and as long as the Lord leaves me my voice, I will use it to give Him glory!"

Her clear eyes met mine, and we rejoiced in the kindred Spirit of the Lord.

"Everything happened after I prayed," I explained. "Shirley got up and changed the songs to gospel, then she gave the microphone to you…"

"And who do you think sent Shirley over to give me that microphone?" she asked with a beatific smile.

"The Lord did, to show His power! He is King of heaven and earth, yes He is!"

I'm glad I met Josefa in this season. She and her faith were more mature than spring or summer, too vibrant for winter. Like the New England fall, this century-old friend of Jesus displayed a beauty so rich she glowed, and all who saw it were changed.

"I will praise you as long as I live, and in Your name I will lift up my hands."
(Psalm 63:4)

November 11, 2009

Juanita was sick, real sick. She had been home for over a week and the kids at the Day Home for Disabled Children missed her. Juanita herself was disabled, paraplegic from an auto accident which had damaged her spinal cord. She got around in a motorized wheelchair, speeding down the dirt road between her house and the orphanage.

"You're like Evel Knieval in that thing!" I told her once. "Aren't you afraid of falling?"

She smiled and told me, "I'm okay! I wear this strap over my knees to keep me from sliding forward."

Five days a week she taught the older students in the program, but her most important lesson to these children, also wheelchair-bound, was her productive life. She was mature in her faith, humble and soft-spoken, yet disciplined and purposeful. Children and adults around the mission loved and respected her.

I had been visiting her at her home where her aunt and cousins helped care for her. A couple of episodes of difficulty breathing had frightened her and now, even though improving, she was discouraged.

"I don't want to be a burden on my family," she confided. "and I want to get back to work. I miss the kids!"

Never one to wallow in self-pity, she focused on Jesus and Scripture to lift herself up.

On Thursday, all the children at the day home made get-well cards for her and Mary asked me, "Do you think it would be all right if we took the kids to visit Juanita?"

They were special beacons of God's love and light. These children touched lives with their sweet spirits and for Juanita, they would be heaven's therapy. We piled them into their van and drove the short distance to their beloved teacher's home. We caught Juanita by surprise as she sat outside under a guava tree, enjoying one of her first outdoor excursions.

"Hola, Juanita!" yelled one child after another. *"Te extrañamos!"* ("We miss you!")

She was someone who guards her emotions and some might have missed it for her lack of expression. But behind her quiet face I recognized an unexpected fullness of joy. These extraordinary children in their radiance of love and goodness had brought the kingdom of God to a poor dusty part of earth.

Dr. Paul Brand, in his book, *In His Image,* wrote about "the paradox that those who seemingly had least reason to be grateful to God showed His love best." On this day some of those who seemingly had the least reason to be grateful to God showed His love to another who seemed also to have little reason for thanks, and the Lord was in their midst. The blessing splashed all over me, filling me with such joy that the only reasonable response was to give thanks to God.

> *"Then will the lame leap like a deer,*
> *and the mute tongue shout for joy…*
> *and the ransomed of the Lord will return.*
> *They will enter Zion with singing;*
> *everlasting joy will crown their heads.*
> *Gladness and joy will overtake them,*
> *And sorrow and sighing will flee away."*
> (Isaiah 35:6, 9-10)

Kids Surround Juanita

November 20, 2009
"We will achieve no harm."

I read this bumper sticker while jogging past a parked white truck.

With nothing else to do, I thought about that message for the next mile or so.

How bland life would be if causing no harm were our highest aspiration! First of all, no one could achieve it. The consequences of every sin harms the earth or its people at least a little.

Only Jesus, in all of history, did no harm and only in Him can our harmful choices be transformed into abundant life.

Saturday, for me, was a marathon of errands. I had jogged, shopped for groceries, had my hair cut, lunched with friends, cashed some checks, bought a dress for a friend's wedding, browsed a farmer's market, picked up donations from two locations and bought clinic supplies at the 99-cent store. Still rushing to meet Kathy for dinner and tired in mind and body, I was not "living in the moment" as Jesus did. I did manage to put my purchases into the trunk but neglected to remove my purse from the shopping cart. My mind who-knows-where, I just drove away. The big brown bag must have looked like an abandoned baby in the seat of the cart.

Many people ask me, "Aren't you scared to live in Mexico with so much crime going on?"

In two years I have not been robbed of even a peso, but during the seven or eight minutes it took me to realize what I'd done and drive frantically back, someone had already helped himself to my purse. Some Christians may have responded with faith and grace. Others who didn't believe in God, still may have reacted in an accepting manner according to their level of emotional maturity. I, however, fell apart – crying in public with such despair that a few people asked if they could help.

"No, thanks! Somebody stole my purse and I had five hundred dollars in it and credit cards, nursing license, everything!"

The good Samaritans showed genuine compassion although they were probably relieved to hear that no one had died. My dear friend, Kathy, took me out to dinner after searching through the rubbish containers and dumpster.

"Does Enrique know?" she asked.

"No, I can't call Mexico, but he'll be fine, probably tell me, 'Be encouraged, Ellie! God is in control! Praise Him in all things!'"

Sixty seconds later, my husband called. I put the phone on "speaker" and Kathy and I smiled as he told me, "Be encouraged, Ellie! Nothing happened! God has control and we need to praise Him!"

Sunday morning I chose to act out my faith, at last.

"Thank you, Lord!" I said aloud in my car. "The money really doesn't matter if I can just see You in all this!"

It pleased me to find that I really meant it. And with this little morsel of faith, the Lord began to work. In church, our choir sang about Jesus "saving, helping, loving, guiding" and the knowledge of His care replaced the last trace of worry. Standing beside my friend, Carol, as we waited to help with the collection, I told her what had happened. She held her head down like she was going to cry, then she said, "I want to give you some money to help"

Since I had no ID to cash a check, she went herself and got cash and came back with two hundred dollars in a little purse. The joy I felt went beyond her gift - the Lord *was* saving, helping, loving, guiding!

Other friends took me out to lunch and chipped in to ease my loss. The next day the bank teller told me, "You're eligible for a new credit card that gives you rewards. There's no monthly fee and the first time you use the card, we'll give you a hundred dollars!"

The Lord completed the reimbursement as I drove back towards Tijuana. Nancy, who keeps track of my donations, called to say someone else was donating a hundred dollars after hearing about the crime. There it was – all the money I'd lost plus a little more, which covered my DMV fees– my God thinks of everything!

So harm was done, to me and to the guilty soul who took my purse. But God used His body: Kathy, Enrique, members of my church, and turned it into abundant life. At the end of the sermon, Pastor Mike asked us to pray for someone who needed healing, and the Lord stirred me to pray with compassion for the person rejoicing over my five hundred bucks but in need of so much more.

"We will achieve no harm?" Impossible goal for either a thief or a whiner like me. Yet thanks be to God for letting me see His kingdom on earth! Harm transformed into abundant life, now *that's* a bumper sticker!

"*For where your treasure is, there your heart will be also.*"

(Matt. 6:21)

December 3, 2009

The light of the mission flickered but did not go out. Javier, who suffers from Muscular Dystrophy, is critically underweight, and came down with a flu and pneumonia, survived. We'd prayed him through illnesses before but this was the worst.

"He woke up coughing so hard I thought we were going to lose him!" Mary told me one morning. "He can't eat because of it and he's so weak, he wouldn't let Dirk do the chest therapy!"

The same therapy, which we knew, was keeping him alive. We'd percuss him gently on the back to loosen up infected secretions which his cough, though constant, was too weak to do. He was lying on Mary's couch when I went in.

"Hola, amor!"

I greeted him as "my love."

Usually Javier had a great sense of humor. He would often answer this kind of greeting with sarcasm, saying something like:

"Kiki, tu amor," reminding me I had chosen my husband, "Kiki," over him.

But I would remind him he would always be my *"otro amor!"* and, satisfied, he'd answer, *"Si!"*

But that morning, there was no play in him. The flatness of his tone when he whispered back, *"Hola,"* frightened me. His exam showed fever, ominous sounds in both lungs and a body rail thin and weaker by the day. Using the formula to figure one's Body Mass Index (BMI), someone is considered underweight if their BMI is 18 or lower. I calculated Javier's at 11, which put him in the category of "living-by-God's-grace-alone." (Of course, we're all in this category but the point is Javier's physical state should not have allowed him to live.)

He got worse and was taken by ambulance in respiratory distress to the General Hospital in Ensenada.

Mary, Dirk and I met with his family and gave them a "hospice" talk.

"Javier is at the point now where we have to consider the burden versus the benefit of everything we do to him or for him!"

We cried and entered into several days of desperate waiting soaked in prayer.

"Lord, we know he's yours and would be better off with you, but we ask selfishly for You to grant us more time with him!"

And the Lord said, "Yes!" After ten days he was pronounced "better" and released. His first day back at the mission, I sat next to him in sala. The speaker read aloud the following verse from Isaiah 9:2:

"The people walking in darkness have seen a great light; on those living in the land of the shadow of death

a great light has dawned."

These words could have been written about my young friend, who modeled true faith and joy in the midst of his burden and brought light into many hearts. He gave me a smile none could match - sincere, innocent, full of gladness and warmth. I hugged him as hard as his emaciated frame could bear and he responded simply,

"Hola, Ellie!"

Scripture itself could not have touched me more deeply. Our poster child had gained a victory. Satan's grip had been loosened by prayer, and all who saw it gave glory to God.

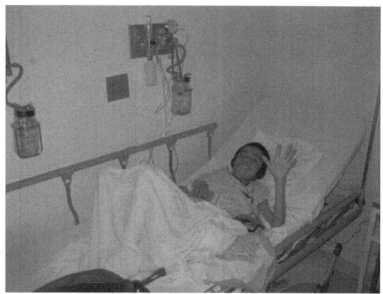

Javier Feeling Better In Hospital

December, 2009
"Silent night, holy night..."

The song we have sung for centuries rises above other Christmas carols for the mystical peace it carries. Its essence is the place we yearn for at Christmas but never quite find. How many times have we vowed to go to less parties, buy fewer gifts, make the holiday simpler, and yet the weeks before are never silent and rarely holy! Enrique and I acted in the mission's annual "Noche En Belen," (Night In Bethlehem) a drama of Christ's life from birth to resurrection. We did more than a dozen shows in three nights, emceed a friend's wedding the next day, attended a Pastor's Dinner, a bible school party, staff Christmas party, went caroling to migrant camps, plus my work and his school. On my "free" day last weekend I drove up and did my Christmas shopping at the San Ysidro Outlet Mall.

"Be still, and know that I am God."(Ps. 46:10)

The only time I have been still lately is during my morning prayer. "Centering Prayer," which I practice, is a method of silent prayer in which we let go of thoughts, desires, everything, so that we may receive God's presence within us. If and when the Lord grants us this supreme gift, it is known as contemplative prayer, something unachievable by our own efforts, given only by His grace. When it occurs, we can exclaim like the psalmist:

*"I have seen You in the sanctuary
and beheld Your power and Your glory.
Because Your love is better than life,
My lips will glorify You."*
(Ps. 63:2-3)

In my bilingual bible, there are times when words in one language have a different connotation than in the other. Psalm 27 gives an example where I much prefer the Spanish. The one thing King David asks of the Lord is to dwell with Him forever and, *"to gaze upon the beauty of the Lord and to seek Him in His temple."* The Spanish word used for "gaze" is *contemplar.* Webster's defines contemplation as "a state of mystical awareness of God's being." It's more than a gaze, it's an awareness we all want - though at first, it's overwhelming.

The story in Luke 5 where Jesus helps Peter out with his fishing can serve as a parable for this state of prayer. The Lord told Peter, *"Put out into deep water, and let down the nets for a catch."* (v. 5) If our goal is to contemplate God, we will need to go to a deep place and "let down our nets" of busy thoughts, selfish desires, and all our plans, good or bad. Peter had *"worked hard all night"* and caught nothing as we do when we pray without the Holy Spirit, and God eludes us. But now, because Christ told him, Peter let down the nets *and "caught such a large number of fish that their nets began to break."*

Ah, the blessings that come when God rushes into our senses! Not the petty things we might request when we pray like a child making his list for Santa, no, this is pure joy, that of knowing the Holy of holies is within us!

Then, like Peter, we might signal our old partners to come to our aid as this unveiled Presence breaks through all our "ideas" of God. We seek help from partners like self-righteousness, justification through good deeds, or intellectualization of the experience of our true self, naked before the Lord. But God's beauty overwhelms all these "boats" and we begin to sink. In that pure Light, we can not help but recognize our own sinfulness.

"Go away from me, Lord; I am a sinful man!"(v. 8)

Immediately, Jesus tells us the same He told Peter,

"Don't be afraid!"

So we stay, letting down our last net, which is fear. Now we can "gaze" upon the Lord, contemplating His beauty, and know the love that is better than life. This is the silent night, the holy night we have been seeking. We are now mangers in which Christ can be born and we carry the peace and joy of His birth into a hurting world.

Thomas Merton, a Trappist monk who spent years in silent prayer, wrote this about the spiritual life: "It is the silence of our whole being in compunction and adoration before God, in the habitual realization that He is everything and we are nothing ...that our life and strength proceed from Him, that all our plans and spiritual ambitions are useless unless they come from Him and end in Him and that, in the end, the only thing that matters is His glory."

"Glory to God in the highest,
and on earth peace to men on whom His favor rests."
(Luke 2:14)

Noche En Belen

Joseph's Parents Dance

Tales of A Five-Star Missionary

December 23, 2009

Except for God, nothing is certain. We learn one thing then science proves another. We take a stand and then are persuaded toward another point of view. In ministry to the poor, I'm convinced the best way to serve them is through education, training of skills, discipleship – anything that empowers and enlightens them to be able to help themselves. I spend half my time explaining, in love, why I'm NOT giving patients medicine and what they can do to get better without it.

The old missionary mentality of doling out food, money, clothes, has been shown to create dependency. (For more on this read Glenn Schwartz's book, *When Charity Destroys Dignity*.) So I do not hand out money, especially in a clinic where, if the word got out, we'd have people lined up for miles to tell us their needs.

Margarita was an exception.

"My head hurts when my blood pressure goes up," she told me.

"Your blood pressure is 124/71. That's not high; it's normal! Did a doctor tell you you had high blood pressure in the past?"

"No, but I can feel it surge into my head when I get angry and then my head aches."

With a smile, I gave her obvious counsel, "My recommendation is that you get angry less!"

We laughed a little, then I said, "Seriously, if you're angry a lot, there is something causing you stress, maybe someone in your life you have not forgiven."

"Well, yes, my husband," she answered without hesitation.

"Does he abuse you?"

"No, he left me for another woman two years ago! It still bothers me. I have four children and there's no work."

She was desperate and telling the truth. Single abandoned mother, no money or work, Christmastime and cold at night. It was one of those times when evangelizing seemed too pat, a "Have a nice day!" kind of message to someone for whom that was impossible. The verses in James came to me: *"Suppose a brother or sister is without clothes and daily food. If one of you says to him, "Go, I wish you well; keep warm and well-fed,' but does nothing about his physical needs, what good is it?"* (James 2:15-16)

Of course, Jesus is always important so I did settle the fact that she knew the Lord and attended a Christian church.

But I acknowledged, "Margarita, I can't tell you that if you pray, God will bring you a job and money. He can and He may, but we don't know! What we do know is that this life is short and the only thing that matters is trusting in God. The bible says there were giants of faith who did not receive what they longed for before they died. But where are they now? Living forever with no tears, no problems, and great, great joy!"

She answered the way the poor often do – with a show of faith that made me think she'd have a greater mansion than mine in heaven.

"Yes, sister, I know! I pray to the Lord when I'm feeling desperate and He consoles me. He is my only hope and I trust in Him! But it's so hard to be alone and see my children hungry!"

What was stopping me from ending the visit with prayer and Tylenol? The Holy Spirit nudged me and I grabbed my purse from under the desk.

"Look, Margarita, I never do this and please, don't ever tell anyone! But I want to bless you with this."

The five hundred pesos I pressed into her hand was worth about forty-three dollars.

"Oh, hermana! Gracias, gracias, oh Dios mio...!"

She held me tight, trembling and crying and thanking God until finally I pried myself loose.

"Buy some Christmas presents for your children, and no candy!" (We had talked about nutrition, too.)

She left still crying and blessing me, my family, my non-existent children and anyone else in my lineage. It took me a few minutes to compose myself then I went over to the office, having received a message to come.

"You have to sign for your bonus," Celina told me.

"What bonus?"

"A Christmas bonus," she replied.

In my two years at the mission, they'd never given bonuses. But here were eighty-four dollars, twice as much as I'd given Margarita. What a God we have! His "Secret Santa" style of giving blessed me the most, the money a distant second.

I still believe that, for the most part, charity destroys dignity and creates dependency, but if King David and his men could eat the bread from the temple and Jesus healed on the Sabbath, I can give away money when the Lord leads me!

Praise be to God Whose love is greater than the law!

2010

January 1, 2010

Armando died on Christmas day. Enrique got a phone call and told me, "He was a pastor, a friend, and part of my formation. Let's stop by the service on Sunday."

The church was simple, set up in the hills of Ensenada. Cars, pickups and vans lined both sides of the dirt road, parked wherever they could to avoid potholes and rocks. We found a space several blocks away and walked back. Mourners spilled out of the church onto the patio and street. There was a predominance of men, gathered in clusters with obvious fellowship.

Inside, every seat was taken and people lined the walls. Armando lay in a white casket, top half open, dressed in a suit with a black felt hat on his chest.

"Why the hat?" I whispered to my husband.

Expecting a cultural explanation, Enrique's simple answer, "He always wore it," touched me.

I wished I had known this man. Delivered out of heroin addiction, he'd become a pastor and director of a rehab center. Many of the young and middle-aged men present had been blessed by counsel, discipleship and tough support from the man who had worn the black hat. Dead at age forty-eight.

"Where's his wife?" I asked.

"There, with the child," said Enrique, motioning with his chin.

She sat in the front row, their large four-year old son asleep against her breast; a sturdy pleasant-looking woman with long softly-curled hair. Susy appeared the perfect complement for a humble busy man of God, with an inner strength and serenity that bore their way up through her agony to bring light and peace to her being. She focused on the pastor's words as though the telling of her husband's life could impart life again.

"Everyone, whether adult or child, teenager or elderly, will at some point have to open that door that leads into the presence of Jesus, and all that will remain is our fruit! Armando is gone but many here today can testify to the fruit he produced."

"I'm a part of that fruit," Enrique said softly.

The pastor continued and the room began to shimmer with the presence of the Holy Spirit. Barriers of time and separateness melted away and we were one, all of us caught up in the truth of the eulogy of the dead man's life.

"We are co-creators of our own future," I wrote on a scrap of paper. It was something to be remembered in life. With every decision, every good or bad deed, with our prayers and faith or lack of them, we fashion our future. Armando decided at a young age to use heroin. His choice damaged his heart and he died at forty-eight. Somewhere in between he decided to stop doing drugs and follow Jesus. Therefore, his eternal future will be spent in heaven with His Savior. Many other choices he made helped create better futures for himself, his family, and countless struggling addicts.

I thought about our diet. Whatever we put in our mouth today, we help create our future health or diseases. If we choose junk, laden with sugar and fats, we create a future which may include cancer, diabetes, obesity and heart disease. Parents fashion those same diseases in their children's lives by allowing them mountains of lollipops, candy and unhealthy snacks.

We can forgive someone today and create a future free of emotional and spiritual bondage. The New

Year is a time to learn a skill, do daily exercise, visit those in prison, show great love, all of which will improve our futures and those of others. But always we face the ultimate decision, the one that matters most - what will we do today with Jesus Christ? Believe in Him? Follow Him? Obey Him? May your future be full of righteousness and blessing!

"Now choose life, so that you and your children may live and that you may love the Lord your God, listen to His voice, and hold fast to Him."
(Deut. 31:19-20)
Consider the blameless, observe the upright There is a future for the man of peace."
(Psalm 37:10-11, 37)

January 19, 2010

I am not a journalist. My stories don't come from interviews, nor do they treat people and events outside my experience. However, the unity of our mission team made others' stories my own and here are two.

Our first outreach was to a community which was a two-hour drive into the mountains outside Oaxaca City. The town had a serene ambience which seemed to originate from both its snug location in the hills and from the people themselves. Not that poverty didn't exist here, but it had not eroded family values nor social peace. The mayor, Honorio, a Christian man, had contributed to this. In fact, he was so beloved by his constituents that they had changed a law limiting terms of office just to allow him to continue to serve.

Monrovio and his family, who once had proclaimed Jesus as their Savior, had moved outside this peace and their life was anything but serene. The young son, in the demonic grip of alcohol and violence, had tried to commit suicide recently. When that failed, he came home drunk one evening and began an argument. In an explosion of rage, he beat his own father then ran away in shame and torment.

Later, a cousin searched and found him, two days sober and sullen.

"There's a team of Christian doctors in town," he told Monrovio. "Come with me and we'll ask them to pray for you!"

"Okay, but I don't want to go with a pastor!" he replied.

Apparently, Monrovio didn't realize that God could use any obedient Christian to pastor a stray sheep. He chose Roberto, our trip leader, and Jose Luis, the men's' deacon from our Bible Institute, not by coincidence, men with their own history of alcoholism but now strong in God's grace.

"I feel like no one loves me," he admitted.

Jose Luis led him to the words of Jesus in John 10:10: *"The thief comes only to steal and kill and destroy; I have come that they may have life, and have it to the full."*

He explained to Monrovio that Satan wanted to steal his family, love, even his life - all that God wanted to give. Then Roberto asked Jose Luis to share the story of the prodigal son, showing that the devil had not done anything new and certainly nothing which God could not repair.

By now, Monrovio's father had joined them and also received counsel and prayer. In the power of the Holy Spirit, he embraced his son and forgave him. Then the mother, two sisters and a brother came and the Spirit of the Lord overcame them all. They hugged and reconciled one with another and left as a family, united and content.

- -

The other story involved Enrique, my husband, and a man whose wife tried to kill him. We had set up clinic in the men's section of the largest prison in Oaxaca. Gregorio had come because of chronic pain in his face and neck. He was hard to look at; his wife had struck him twenty times with a machete, gouging out one eye and disfiguring him completely.

"I was in the hospital for two months and when I got out, I didn't remember anything! Everyone was amazed that I survived. My neighbors asked me, 'Why did she do that to you?' 'Who? Do what?' I asked."

"Your wife," they told me. "She tried to kill you!"

"So I went to where she lived. But as soon as she saw me, she called the police and they came and arrested me! I've already been here eighteen months and my sentence is eight years!"

"Have you forgiven her?" Enrique asked.

He did not ask the question lightly, for he had had the experience of forgiving the man who murdered his sister.

"The hardest thing I ever did," he told Gregorio, "but the Lord forgave me and in order to be free, I also had to forgive a man I wanted to kill."

With prayer and testimony and the word of God, Gregorio received Jesus into his heart and pardoned his wife.

"He began to cry," Enrique told me. "I saw tears coming down his cheek but there was no eye, only the tears!"

It will be the opposite in heaven. Gregorio will have eyes that see the beauty of the Lord, but no tears.

"The Sovereign Lord will wipe away the tears from all faces;
He will remove the disgrace of His people from all the earth.
The Lord has spoken.
In that day they will say,
"Surely this is our God;
we trusted in Him, and He saved us."
(Isaiah 25:8-9)

January 21, 2010

My purpose as part of the team in Oaxaca was to teach - about health, about Jesus, or whatever the Lord put on my heart. To empower and set people free through knowledge of disease prevention and the gospel. My passion.

The first village, Chicomezulchi, was the one where Honorio, a Christian man, was mayor. The ambience of this community was peaceful and the children, well-behaved. In the afternoon, when this younger generation attached itself to me, I demonstrated oral care, hand washing, and taught about the harm of eating too much sugar. But earlier, in the morning, when only a dozen little ones had arrived, I seated them around a plastic table and gave them crayons and paper.

"Draw your life as it is right now! Draw how you spend an average day, the good, the bad, everything!"

They set to work. Peeking over their shoulders, I saw lots of children at play, parents with their young, and perfect houses with tiny birds flying overhead under sun and puffy clouds. An art therapist would have scored them emotionally healthy.

"Tell me about yours, Pedro!" I began.

"This is me and this is my family. We're playing."

"The big ones are your parents?"

"Yes," he said.

"So you're playing outside with your parents?"

"Yes."

"And do you really do that, play with your parents?"

Again, an affirmative.

Wow! I had expected hints of the misery and hopelessness of poverty to be the theme of their pictures. Instead my heart applauded these parents who took time to enjoy their children. How many first-world families "play outside together?" Not on the same computer or on the couch watching TV, but outdoors, running, exploring, breathing the same air and life?

Many of the children had drawn similar simple but pleasant images. Then I told them, "On the other half of the page, draw how you'd like your future to be! The future of your dreams, whatever you want!"

The purpose of this exercise was to get them to dream, then perhaps, to plan. Too many sons and daughters around the world assume their lives will be replicas of their parents'. With vision and planning they could design a better life than working in the fields, struggling for food, and aging prematurely by exposure to the elements and bad nutrition.

When the children had drawn their futures, there were a few who envisioned themselves as professionals. One boy, thirteen years old, drew himself sitting at a computer.

"What are you doing at the computer?" I asked.

"I want to learn about better ways to farm then come back and teach people!"

I almost fell down. He had verbalized the dream manner of development, the poor themselves figuring out their highest needs, empowering themselves through education and skills training, then using it to lift up their own communities.

Most of the others had drawn pictures almost identical to the one of their lives at present, but with their own children added in. Still, not an unpleasant life, on paper.

"Give your drawing to the person on your right and we're going to pray that these futures come true!"

The kids laid hands on their friends' lives and prayed earnestly. Then each took back his own and I told them, "Take them home and continue to pray." I prayed for them, also.

"Give them dreams, Lord, great ones! And let them know You, the giver of every good thing. Let them seek the future You have for each one, a future of blessing and not of harm. Raise them up, dear Lord, so they may bring Your great light into the world's darkness. I give them to You, O Lover of Children, for their care and protection and fruit! Amen!"

When Enrique walked by, I asked him to lead the children in a prayer to invite Christ into their hearts. Hand in hand with my husband, encircled by twenty or more little ones, I listened while they repeated Enrique's words, not feebly, but with the power to open Heaven. In that moment I knew I was doing exactly what I had been designed to do. Joy and peace rushed in, gifts of the Holy Spirit. It was what I wanted for all children, rich or poor, to align their lives with God's design and enjoy, enjoy their Savior and His blessing.

"But seek first His kingdom and His righteousness, and all these things will be given to you as well." (Matt. 6:33)

Tales of A Five-Star Missionary

Praying For His Future

Brushing Teeth

January 24, 2010

Every time we visited a prison I had two thoughts:
1. *To be confined in such a place would drive me insane,* and
2. *How easily I could have ended up here had Christ not changed my life!*

Such musings fuelled my compassion for the female inmates, some barely out of their teens with long sentences, their futures dismal.

"We've arranged a classroom for you to meet with the women," Roberto told me. "There'll be a social worker for security."

This "security" was laughable, a young lady, probably just out of college, sat in the far corner of the front row of desks. I felt more in common with the ten inmates. A male guard closed the door from the outside and we had privacy uncommon in prison.

What shall I teach? I wondered. Diabetes, high blood pressure, nutrition? As quickly as I thought of these, I dismissed them. They would put me in the category of the social worker – separate and irrelevant.

"Why don't we start with each person telling your name, where you come from and what family you have!"

CHE (Community Health Evangelism) training had taught me the importance of class participation but my real motive was more basic: I wanted to know them.

"Guadalupe, Esperanza, Piedad, Lupita, two children, three, five, four."

All had kids, none mentioned their marital status. They mentioned that seven of them had been moved here at four in the morning from another prison. No warning, no time to gather clothes or toiletries. The worst, though:

"Our families don't know where we are!"

A glance at the social worker told me she had no opinion or information she wanted to share, so I empathized and moved on. The Holy Spirit guided me. A short version of my testimony knocked down some walls as they saw this was not some lily-white *gringa*. We put on a CHE drama about holistic health, changing the main character of *Senor Lopez* to *Senora*. They laughed a lot even while learning humans are created body, mind and soul, and a person with a vengeful heart is not healthy.

Then we moved on to the first part of the Health Education Program for Developing Countries. (hepfdc.org)

"The most important knowledge we have about health is that God loves us and we ought to love one another! By loving and forgiving each other, we may avoid headaches, high blood pressure, stomach distress, mental disorders, heart disease, cancer, and abusive relationships!"

To be in a setting where abuse could be talked about freely was a gift. After defining it and again sharing my own experience, I asked,

"How many of you have ever been in an abusive relationship?"

Every woman except the social worker raised her hand.

"You need to forgive that person - father, husband, boyfriend, alive or dead! If you want to be free, you must forgive!"

Finally I talked about how Jesus could help them do what was impossible, to forgive someone who had treated them badly, and to be free even inside prison.

"Will you pray for us who were moved last night?"

"Yes, gladly, and then whoever wants to wait, I'll pray for individually."

Half of them waited, talking with each other while I ministered to individuals. Four invited Jesus into their hearts. Many denied committing the crime they were sentenced for. We read Bible verses that showed God's hatred of oppression and injustice and encouraged them to let Him be their judge, truth, and light.

Then I rejoined our team in the clinic. Guadalupe, a forty-year old who had just accepted Christ, sat with me while she waited to see the doctor.

"Read the Bible!" I encouraged her. "God will talk to you through it. Read the psalms and share all your emotions with Him! Use them as your prayers!"

We turned to Psalm 25 and she read aloud:

"Show me Your ways, O Lord, teach me Your paths;
guide me in Your truth and teach me,
for You are God my Savior, and my hope is in You all
day long."

"Wow!" she said with an innocent smile. "Can you show me another one?"

She was hungry for the word of God, so we searched the Scriptures together, equally amazed by the power and tenderness of the Lord.

Each woman had written her name on a piece of paper at the beginning of our "class." They are still in my Bible and I pray for my little flock by name.

"I will heal their waywardness and love them freely, for
my anger has turned away from them."
(Hosea 14:4)

February 2, 2010
"The rain in Spain falls mainly on the plain."

In Baja it falls mainly on the poor. Not to say the rich didn't get drenched, too, in last week's storm, but our suffering was limited mostly to wet boots and runny mascara. Whereas the three-day deluge melted snow in the mountains and created an ocean of water that rushed into the valley and ravaged flimsy homes in its path.

I stood in the front yard of a dwelling that had a direct view of the mountains across flat farmland.

"Could you see the water coming?"

Leticia, thirteen, answered me.

"Oh yes! It came across the field like the sea, with big waves! We didn't have time to take anything, we just ran back and back to where it stopped. When we could return, the house was filled with mud!"

The river bed that runs through our community of Vicente Guerrero rose with the storm and ran with such fury, the cement bridge collapsed and water lines snapped, isolating whole communities and depriving them of safe water, food, and propane.

The mission went into relief mode, delivering meals and fresh water to villages which had none. One leather-skinned grandmother carted two five-gallon jugs, and after we filled them, she walked far down the road towards home, balancing the load in her wheelbarrow. Dorothy, the mission's baker, made huge loaves of bread and gallons of soup, and we handed them out, still warm, to the hungry.

"I heard little Jose's house was flooded," said Mary, speaking of one of her handicapped children. "We're going to try to visit them."

Dirk was driving the four-wheel drive Suburban and forged through deep puddles and long streets of mud. But in Jose's neighborhood, the deluge had been so severe the entire area - homes, yards, roads - were buried in mire. After making it through several rough spots, we got hopelessly stuck in knee-deep sludge. Dirk got out and tried to free us, the muck reaching within an inch of the top of his rubber boots. He scooped it away from the tires with bare hands and commanded the rest of us, "Don't get out!" With some guilt I say the eight of us, dry inside the vehicle, were glad to obey.

When it was clear we couldn't get loose, some local men came to our rescue. They dug, pushed, deliberated, and finally used a truck and chain to tow us out.

At one point during all this, I opened the door of the car. From my point of dry comfort, I spoke to a man standing calf-deep in mud.

"Do you have mud in your house?" I asked.

"The whole house, up to here," he answered, drawing an imaginary line at knee level.

"What are you going to do?"

"I don't know," he said.

His response held no note of despair, just truth. Yet he was here, helping us.

When he returned to the task, I told my friends inside the car, "You know, we just passed two of these men who are helping Dirk. They were carrying out muddy mattresses from a house and stacking them up in the front yard to dry!" "Yes, and a couple who came already had shovels! I'm sure they were busy digging out their own houses," said Jack, a visitor.

Mary and I had an edge on the short-term visitors with us. We were already familiar with the generosity of the poor. Yet in these stark conditions, where people who had so little had lost even that, where food, clothes and water were unfulfilled desires, still, they had dropped everything and run to our aid. Everything was upside down. We were supposed to be the rich, the ones giving the help; instead we sat, rescued by those we had come to save.

The next day, we visited Zaida, another of our disabled children, and found her mom cooking for the family over a small fire she'd made in the yard. Though her own family lacked propane and was down to two liters of potable water, Fausta had taken in an abused friend and her two babies.

"When my husband was on drugs and abusing me, no one helped me, not even my family. I know what it's like so if I can help my friend, I will!"

The house had only one room. Two women and five girls shared a queen-size bed while Fausta's husband and son shared the only other piece of furniture, a twin bed.

"I hope no one snores!" I joked.

"If they do, they're out!" Fausta informed us.

Then, Sunday, I visited my home church, Solana Beach Presbyterian. Pastor Mike spoke about giving.

"The rich young ruler went away sad because he could not give up his possessions, but the poor old widow put in all that she had. It's not the size, but the sacrifice of giving."

I remembered all the heroes whom I'd seen give out of their poverty.

Mike read 1 Timothy 6:17-19.

"Command those who are rich in this present world not to be arrogant nor to put their hope in wealth, which is so uncertain, but to put their hope in God, Who richly provides us with everything for our enjoyment. Command them to do good, to be rich in good deeds, and to be generous and willing to share...so that they may take hold of the life that is truly life."

No such command is addressed to the poor, perhaps because they already understand the hopelessness of this world and their dependency on one another. They feel the urgent need for a Savior! It would have been cruel to tell Zaida's mom, her abused friend, or the displaced persons that God "provides everything for our enjoyment." Still, isn't the pleasure those men got from helping us or Fausta's joy in being able to offer shelter to a friend, aren't these enjoyments God provides?

The longer I live among the poor, the more they teach me how to live. May we who are rich let go of that which moths and rust, rains and mud can destroy and instead, every day, "take hold of the life that is truly life."

Dirk in the Mud

Our Rescuers

Zaida (lavendar jacket), Mom (far right), her friend (far left) and others who share one bed

February 26, 2010

God has opened a new door for me and it's thrilling for me to walk through it. When the Board of Directors here at FFHM, (Foundation For His Ministry) created the new position as "Nurse Educator," they gave me both opportunity and responsibility. There is a world of knowledge available which, if put into practice, can improve quality of life, maintain health, and empower the poor.

Understanding the importance of breastfeeding and dangers of formula is a crucial part of this path. So the Lord sent me Amy, a visitor from Wisconsin.

She told me, "I know you like to teach women about breastfeeding and I'd like to help you!"

Turned out, she was expert in the topic through both experience and research. Dr. Arnie Gorske, a world health expert and my mentor in ministry, told me many times, "If you nurses could convince women to breastfeed their babies for two or three years, you'd save more lives than any doctor!"

Here was our chance. Working with our "Outreach" department, we arranged to present the information in a different location each day. I began the talk with a visual. Holding up a water pistol in one hand and a baby bottle in the other, I asked the group, "What do these two things have in common?" When nobody guessed correctly I gave the answer.

"They both kill people."

Now they were listening.

"We all know that guns kill people but how many realize that one million babies die around the world every year because they're bottle fed! One reason is that babies who receive breast milk have better immune systems and if they get sick, they can recover more easily. But babies who only drink formula often die from the same sickness!"

Two women in the circle opened their shirts and put their little ones to the breast.

"The other reason so many die is that the bottles of formula are rarely prepared in a sterile manner. The bottle and the formula can grow germs which cause diarrhea and vomiting that may lead to death."

Amy continued with the many nutritive benefits, the hormonal element which causes mother-infant emotional bonding, and a decreased risk of some cancers and other diseases for moms who nurse their young. She offered one-on-one consultations after we finished and two women came to us with questions.

So much of what she said had spiritual implications.

"Many women stretch their breasts toward the baby, but the best way to nurse is to rest back and pull the baby to your breast."

Neither does God run after us. Rather He draws us to Himself, the Source of all love and nourishment.

Amy told me, "The baby cries because he's uncomfortable but doesn't realize that it's hunger; he just knows some need is not satisfied. But when he finds the breast and receives the milk, he knows it's what he wanted and is content."

And I thought of all the people who are lost, crying in their discomfort with life, but not knowing what they really need. Until that day when they receive Christ. Then they realize He is what they were lacking; He is their comfort, their sustenance, their refuge.

"Can a mother forget the baby at her breast and have no compassion on the child she has born?

Though she may forget, I will never forget you!"

The words of the Lord through the prophet, Isaiah.

Tales of A Five-Star Missionary

What Do These Two Things Have In Common?

My Mommy Gives Me Breast Milk

Tales of A Five-Star Missionary

March 20, 2010

After four days in class during the regional and global CHE conferences, I was ready for more active days of travel. The Evangelical Baptist Missionary Base outside of Managua, where we'd stayed, was a lovely expanse of grassland, trees and comfortable housing. Community Health Evangelism leaders from all over Latin America had shared successes and struggles with transformational ministry and together planned for the future.

Now I had two days to wander the country.

"Go see Grenada! It's lovely; the jewel of Nicaragua!" people told me.

However, I woke up hours before my departure with an achy right eye. Looking in the bathroom mirror, the eye that stared back at me was angry, red, and swollen.

"Oh, great! Now I can't put my contacts in and without them, all I see is one big blur!"

"Don't you have glasses?" my roommates asked.

Obviously, they didn't know about my childhood traumas. Taunts of "four eyes!" and "Hey, Goolkasian, do your glasses steam up when you eat Campbell Soup?" had convinced me never to go out in public wearing my eyeglasses. But at fifty-seven years of age, sanity overruled vanity and on went the coke-bottle spectacles.

Grenada, though not rich, kept its colonial architecture in good repair. Historical buildings painted in lively pastels with white trim served as boutique hotels and decent restaurants. Street vendors sold handicrafts; children begged or sold crude flowers made of palm fronds.

At lunch in a pizzeria, a bulletin inside each menu, in front of the appetizer page, asked in English, "Will you help or hurt a child tonight?" It reported that the children on the streets of Grenada have learned that "tourists are like walking banks that hand out money and food." Many have stopped going to school because begging or selling things is so profitable. Parents force their children into the streets because the kids can earn more in a few hours begging than the adults can make working all day. Easily, these youngsters fall prey to drugs, stealing, and prostitution.

Tales of A Five-Star Missionary

Will You Help or Hurt a Child Tonight?

The children on the streets of Granada begging for food and money has become an epidemic that is destroying children's lives. These children have become taught that tourists are like walking banks that hand out money or food on a whim.

- **THESE KIDS HAVE HOMES...**
  The homeless situation in Granada is not nearly as severe as in other poor cities. Orphanages and charity organizations take care of homeless children. These kids have parents and family.

- **THESE KIDS HAVE FOOD...**
  ...but these kids want the hamburgers, french fries, and other rich foods that the tourists eat. These kids normally eat rice and beans like all other children in Nicaragua– and those that **are** hungry are fed in a large charity kitchen here in Granada called "Carita Feliz" (Happy Face). These kids, however, **refuse** to eat at this kitchen because so many tourists will give them much richer foods. ☞ Carita Feliz (meals and social development): www.caritafeliz.org

- **THESE KIDS BELONG IN SCHOOL...**
  These kids arrive on the street usually attending school and within days drop out and begin spending all their time on the street begging late into the night.
  ☞ La Esperanza Granada (education organization): www.la-esperanza-granada.org

- **THESE KIDS ARE BECOMING DRUG ADDICTS AND PROSTITUTES...**
  The bad influences that these children find every night in the street include drugs, sniffing glue (a deadly activity that very effectively destroys the brain), and child prostitution.

- **THESE KIDS ARE BEING EXPLOITED...**
  Many times these children are sent by their parents to earn money, since the children can earn more begging for a few hours than the parents can working a full day. Some children are beaten if they do not want to beg. Poor, irresponsible men and women will "rent" hungry looking children to use for begging in the streets.
  ☞ Mi Familia (government family assistance program): www.mifamilia.gob.ni

ANYTHING YOU GIVE TO THESE CHILDREN HELPS TO DESTROY THEIR LIVES
♥ PLEASE EXERCISE TOUGH LOVE ♥
GIVE TO A REPUTABLE ORGANIZATION THAT CAN <u>REALLY</u> HELP

I had seen these kids. They roamed the streets day and night with baskets of handicrafts on their heads or bags of small candies for sale. The smallest ones simply stared you down with their World Vision eyes until you released some *cordobas* or a nice American dollar into their outstretched hand.

By evening, my infected eye ached from overuse so the next day I chose a different tactic, inserting my left contact and taping a gauze bandage over the right eye to rest it. By mid-morning the humid heat loosened the tape from my sweaty forehead and the eye patch fell to the ground. I spent the day trying to remember to keep that eye closed, but invariably it would open. The vision was like that of the man Jesus healed with spit - the stage where, *"I see people; they look like trees walking around."*

And like me with one lens, many wealthy tourists have only partial vision. They go to dinner happy because they "gave to the poor."

How we see the developing world depends on us. We can keep one eye shut and see only the palm trees, handicrafts, and photogenic children. With two eyes we can see that the poor don't live in the neat, pastel houses. They live in shacks with neither clean water nor plumbing and earn less than two dollars a day.

My last lunch in Nicaragua was at a restaurant called, El Tercer Ojo or "The Third Eye." The décor was eastern with Hindu influences of goddesses, tapestries and incense. I went simply for the food and it was delicious. Staring at the logo of a huge eye on tapestry, I realized it probably symbolized spiritual vision for the Hindus. What it showed me was that we can have a thousand eyes and still not see.

Jesus told the rich young ruler, "Go, sell everything you have and give to the poor...then come, follow me."

As hard as it is to get the first part right, the "come, follow me" part is the more difficult. Did Christ mean to have a big yard sale, give the proceeds to charity and be done with it? Or did He want the man to unburden himself of everything which kept him from freely following Jesus? Ministries that help transform people's lives are the "follow me" part of Jesus' command. What we need to give to the poor is ourselves. In living beside them, listening to their hearts and ideas, together we can come up with a better way.

Dear Carol,

I am writing to you, the "CHE" representative of the Board of Directors. If our primary concern is for the children, good nutrition must be a part of that concern.

Months ago, I taught food groups and the harmful effects of sugar to all grades at the mission school. At that time I was dismayed to learn we were selling processed sugary junk food out of the school's *tiendita*. I have met with various people but yesterday, I purchased a sample of everything the school is still selling.

One unidentifiable treat in a plastic shell contained: "Sugar, glucose, (highest two ingredients, both sugar) citric acid, artificial color and flavor (known carcinogens), "high red," "brilliant blue," (chemical dyes) and chile. Apparently they don't have the same labeling requirements as the States because most of the other equally harmful snacks had no ingredient list or nutritional info. However I will include a photo to show you they ALL are sugary, processed substances completely devoid of nutrition.

Mexico has recently passed a law banning junk food in schools and requiring that students do sixty minutes of exercise every day.

As Christians, shouldn't we do things better than the world, especially when it comes to caring for our children? Kathy and I are working hard to grow organic fruits and vegetables which the kitchen can use to improve the nutrition in their meals. But if our students are sold sugar and chemicals, they won't be hungry for the more healthy offerings.

The orphanage just received a huge donation from the "Gleanings" organization of dried fruit and we have the largest macadamia tree farm outside of Hawaii. Yet, neither was available in the school's store.

Tales of A Five-Star Missionary

      I just finished reading *Food & Behavior, A Natural Connection*, by Barbara Reed Stitt. She was a Chief Probation Officer and later earned a PhD in nutrition. She studied the relationship between diet and behavior for years and helped many young criminals back to healthy productive lives. The back cover reads: "Ask any hyperactive child, depressed, angry teenager, violent adult or criminal what they eat and you'll find they "live" on junk food – sweetened boxed cereals, candy, carbonated drinks, potato chips, fast foods. Junk food abuses the mind, undernourishes the body and distorts behavior."

      Can we eliminate at once the dangerous snacks from our school, please? Pretty please, with no sugar on top?

      Our kids will be eternally grateful!

Sincerely,

Ellie Goolkasian Lugo   (School Snack Choices)

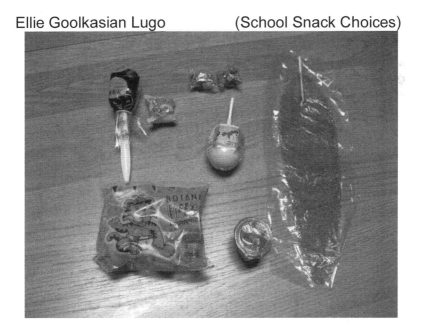

April 23, 2010

My friend, Kathy, has something in common with the First Lady. They both believe that organic gardening is an important means of improving the nutrition and therefore the health of a community. Michelle Obama doesn't get as dirty as Kathy, who digs, hauls, and labors like a twenty-year old man.

The San Quintin Valley is an agricultural area and the use of pesticides is heavy. A hematologist once told me, "I see twice the rate of Leukemia as normal in children from that region."

Kathy's husband, a landscape architect, died from a cancer that began in his tonsils. He had used pesticides for twenty-five years and though his widow kept the business going after his death, she went completely organic. Now God is using her knowledge to help the mission learn to grow seasonal fruits and vegetables pesticide-free.

The design is that it be a holistic project involving various arms of the mission and benefitting all who live here or visit.

"It's not my garden!" Kathy made clear. "If no one takes ownership of it after I leave or if the kitchen doesn't use what we grow, there's no point!"

So we recruited a team. Men from Rancho de Cristo, our rehab center, got rocks from the river and laid them for the garden walls, twenty beds, each four and a half by twenty feet.

My role was to teach everyone the importance of good nutrition, starting with the houseparents and kitchen staff, then the children and missionaries.

Probably the key figure in the project was a teenager named Gabino. This sweet-natured boy had already started working in the fields when he was thirteen. An auto accident did severe damage to one of his legs and he came to the orphanage for wound care.

Once healed, he stayed on for an education. One spring, he discovered his love and gifting for gardening; everything he planted flourished. Of his own accord one Sunday at the beginning of harvest, he presented his first fruits to the Lord in church.

"Gabino's our man," we all agreed. "Kathy can teach him this new style of gardening and he can take over when she leaves!"

Araceli, the kitchen supervisor, was another important personality. She grew up at the orphanage, then was a houseparent for eleven years before transferring to the kitchen. Tales of her multi-faceted experience gave us insight into the orphanage culture, food preferences and habits, and potential roadblocks we might run into. But this remarkable woman gave us a green light and agreed to work with us, with the reminder, "Whatever you grow has to be enough for four hundred people!"

One afternoon, Kathy, Gabino and I stood looking out at the worksite. Eight of the twenty beds had been outlined with rock.

"I know it's different than what you're used to," Kathy told her protégé, "but they require less work than traditional gardens and produce more! The name, "lasagna gardens" came because of the way they're constructed, in layers."

Gabino struggled to accept such a great change in style. And who was this gringa anyway who told him, "First we lay down cardboard and soak it!"

Indeed, the layers start with broken down cartons, which you then saturate to hurry their decomposition. Subsequent layers include grass clippings, straw, compost, seaweed, then more compost. The cardboard stifles the weeds and keeps many bothersome insects out and the vegetables grow in the compost, which is rich and nourishing.

So, here we go! For two health-conscious missionaries with a desire to teach, nourish and unite people, it's a dream project. But like the irrigation system which will water the plants, we need an outpouring of prayer to transform our dream into a harvest.

By faith, we claim John 4:35:

"I tell you, open your eyes and look at the fields! They are ripe for harvest!"

Gabino

Kathy with men from Rancho de Cristo starting the gardens

Tales of A Five-Star Missionary

May 22, 2010

When we're young, we have to beware of friends who draw us into trouble. Still at my age I find this to be true. When Kathy, who's supposed to be my friend and partner, volunteered us to cook for the entire mission, I wanted to pretend I didn't know her.

Araceli, the kitchen supervisor, told us, "You have to plan for three hundred people!"

If we were making peanut butter and jelly sandwiches, maybe I wouldn't have felt like the boy with the five loaves and two fishes for the multitude. At least his was ready to eat!

But Kathy and I already started educating children, staff and the cooks in the importance of healthy nutrition. The new gardens would soon provide organic produce. So the next step was to introduce this new way of eating to everyone - those who would prepare it and those who would consume it.

We began the evening before, armed with Cuisinarts, slicing and dicing onions, chiles and tomatoes. In the morning, we joined the cooks in the kitchen. They were relaxed and jovial, watching this reality show of inexperienced gringas cooking for a Hispanic multitude.

"The salad will be avocados, tomatoes, cucumbers, and jicama," I told the women waiting with their cutting boards and knives.

A couple of them shrugged in a "whatever" gesture; the only salad they were used to was iceberg lettuce and tomatoes. But once we started chopping vegetables in community, our differences dissolved

"Have you ever seen the movie, *Like Water for Chocolate?* I asked Araceli. "Where all the women are spiritually connected by the meal they are preparing?"

It was true. A moment came when my anxiety left and filling the trays with sautéed onions became a holy moment. Kathy, her sister, Linda, the cornbread queen from Tennessee, and I were one with these Mexican sisters preparing a wholesome meal for our large family. I never felt more motherly.

"I don't know why you were so nervous!" I teased Kathy. "This is turning out great!"

Linda, up to her elbows in batter, looked at her sister standing by the stove and rolled her eyes. Tolerating me.

A moment of crisis came when we took the pans out of the oven too soon. As Araceli dug into the casserole to begin serving the salivating crowd, we saw a horrible sight. The cornbread topping was not cooked; spilling over the sides of her huge spatula in a semi-solid yellow mush. My fellow missionaries and darling orphanage kids suddenly took on the look of a lynch mob as we returned the pans to the oven.

"Sorry! We're new at this! Please give us ten more minutes!" I announced with as much calm as I could muster.

Everyone waited. Kathy, Linda and I hid behind the oven for the last three minutes. After that, things went well.

We never did figure out exactly what *Tamale Pie* should be called in Spanish but it didn't matter. Except for a few of the children, everyone ate all they could until it ran out, even the salad, and most gave good reviews!

It's a start. We pray the desire for healthy food will catch on and the revamped menu take hold. Our belief is that as we use God's intended fuel for our bodies, we'll experience better performance and more abundant life!

Kathy and Linda

Linda and I with the Cooks

July 7, 2010

Teaching nutrition in the mission's day home for disabled children was lovely.

That word "lovely" in Webster's has the following definitions:
1. lovable
2. delightful for beauty, harmony, or grace
3. grand, swell
4. eliciting love by moral or ideal worth

When I was deciding if it were the correct word to use, I looked it up, and God used the dictionary to show me all that occurred in the class yesterday.

The day-home was the final group to receive the teaching. I'd shown the powerpoint and taught the information to each of the orphanage "families," encouraging the houseparents to reinforce the knowledge.

Since then, some of the children have come up to me, some proud, some shy, with testimonies such as:

"I don't like junk food!"
"I don't eat too much candy."
"Today I ate salad."

They don't know how they gladdened the heart of Nurse Ellie.

But of all the little ones, those in the disabled program were special to me, my wedding attendants, my light, my ceaseless joy. So I took great pleasure to read the following statement in a blog called *Mission Increase* (missionincrease.org):

"The key to real transformation is not in service, but in kinship. To paraphrase: 'Service of the poor is obvious, it's to be expected. But service is just a hallway that leads to the great banquet hall of kinship.'

Service, as important as it is, can keep us at arm's

length. Service can underscore and even perpetuate the classifications of *us* and *them*..."

Some of the disabled kids have mental capacities below their stated age, and I didn't know if they would be able to grasp my teaching. But any interaction with these darlings blessed me and the blog quote encouraged me that my love and desire to be with them was more than frills; it was the power of God.

"I'm very glad to be here because you are some of my favorite people!" I began.

Javier smiled broadly but shook his head and said, "No!"

It sounded Russian, *"Nyet,"* and was simply his innocent sarcastic humor. I told him, *"Si. Te amo"* (Yes. I love you) and he relented with his own, *"Te amo"* which sounded like *Tamo.*

We talked about the good food that God created and the bad food that man created. We counted out twelve teaspoons of sugar into a glass to show them how much there is in every coke they drink. And we handed out different colored fruits on toothpicks so they could enjoy "God's sweets." When all was said and done, my biggest concern was that they knew how much I loved them.

Later Daniel Webster taught me we truly had had a lovely time, for we'd experienced each definition:
1. lovable – they were, to the extreme.
2. delightful for beauty, harmony, or grace. We had all three: they were beautiful, our souls were in harmony and we felt God's grace. Delightful!
3. grand, swell - It was, for sure.
4. eliciting love by moral or ideal worth. This one is key – their "worth" as children created in the

image and likeness of God elicited love, which surpasses knowledge.

So, yes, I hope they'll eat less sugar, more fruits and vegetables; but more, I hope their souls prosper. After all, it was not service, but kinship I sought. Lovely.

Tales of A Five-Star Missionary

August, 2010

We were on a weekend break of our CHE Internship in the Philippines. Pescador Island was reputed to be one of the top dive sites in the world, so aesthetically, it would have been a choice spot to drown.

We'd hired two Filipino chain-smokers in an outrigger canoe to take us snorkeling. A brilliant coral reef encircled the island; its outer edge formed a two-hundred foot wall, teeming with life. Swimming beyond that, I found myself suspended over a watery abyss. Lasers of sunlight cut through the blue and lit up a roving turtle. The light could not penetrate fully though, so the bottom lay in darkness.

Twinges of fear pecked at me, irrational thoughts that I might fall into the depths. At the same time, I had an almost imperceptible urge to dive into those depths, to enter fully into the unseen. More, it was as though the mystery itself were summoning me.

"Deep calls to deep." (Ps. 42:7)

With a few strong strokes I was back in the shallows where an abundance of attractive fish and coral gardens kept me entertained. I forgot about the deep.

Phil yelled suddenly, "Who wants to circle the island with me?"

"I'll go!" I shouted back.

Kathy and Rob joined us while the others waited in the boat. We set out in a counterclockwise direction, passing over green, yellow and lavender coral heads and the gorgeous display of fish that fed on them. Soon we entered an enormous dark cloud of sardines. The sun caught certain ones at the right angle and glints of silver sparkled in the dark mass. In an instant they passed some secret signal and split apart, creating a hollow chamber the size of a small room and we swam through their midst.

Rounding the corner to the windward side of the island, the chaos began. Choppy waves hit us and the current flowed against us.

"I can't breathe!"

No one heard my yell. Saltwater filled my snorkel, making me cough and gasp. Each time I blew it out, more entered. With calm I could have regulated my breathing. But panic robbed me of such wisdom.

"Are you okay?"

Phil had spotted me and could see I was in trouble.

"No! Can you help me?"

"Come with me! We'll swim to the island."

He half dragged me there, but when we arrived it was too steep and rocky to approach. A wave slammed me into the rock, scraping my hip and elbow.

"Can you climb up onto those steps?" Phil asked.

Again, I answered, "No!"

Some fragment of rationality told me if I took off my diving fins, I'd be able to scramble up between waves but fear said, *what if you slip back into the ocean without them?*

"We better get away from here! It's too dangerous!" I told Phil.

He was tired, too, from fighting the chop and current while trying to hold me up, but he stuck by me. I swam back into the turbulence and immediately had the same struggle for breath. Fear incapacitated me. I kicked and paddled out of synch. My breathing came too fast and poorly timed making me choke and gasp.

During this thrashing, an insane moment of peace swept over me. The thought, *I might die here*, came to my mind but I was not disturbed. That same odd attraction to the deep returned. For the briefest moment,

I considered surrender, to enter the mystery even at the cost of my life.

This madness was, of course, fleeting. When it passed I ordered myself to a calmer state, took some clean breaths and looked around. Kathy and Rob had returned and Phil was still there, my comforter.

One of them yelled, "Tell those boys to come over here!"

Two local youths, not even teenagers, were paddling a canoe nearby. Rob swam in their direction and motioned for them to approach. They were in a small outrigger, with a bamboo beam that floated off one side and stabilized the vessel. When they got close, I thrashed my way toward them and attached myself to their beam. Floating like this, I relaxed, sort of. Quite a bit of adrenaline still surged.

"Thank you so much! Please let me stay here until our boat comes!"

Neither of them understood one word but they were clear the excited lady in the water needed help. Rob got another local boat to go tell our captain to retrieve us and the crisis was over.

For days what I remembered most was that strange desire to just let go. Yet at the decisive moment my whole being fought to stay alive.

This trip has been the most difficult of all my travels. The suffocating heat has made other discomforts - lack of proper toilet and shower, strange food, cultural differences – intolerable. God, in His redeeming way, offered to use these discomforts for growth. He called to me - the voice in the deep - to surrender, to let go of my needs and join Him in the mysterious place where such discomforts took on strange beauty, like the odd creatures in the deepest parts of the ocean. He called me to die to myself and enter more fully into His great love.

And as attractive as was this selflessness, I swam away from its depth and sought with desperation the shallower pleasures: complaining, air-conditioning, fans, and any passing breeze.

So, twice I did not die. Yet God is always faithful. He keeps on blessing me and soon He will call me again to the deep. And perhaps because I'm still sweating in the Philippines and not on an air-conditioned jet to San Diego, I have let go a little.

November 8, 2010

So often the Bible's wisdom takes that of the world and stands it on its head.

"For when I am weak, then I am strong."
(2 Corinth. 12:10)

"If anyone wants to be first, he must be the very last, and the servant of all."
(Mark 9:35)

"Has not God chosen those who are poor in the eyes of the world to be rich in faith and to inherit the kingdom He promised those who love Him?"
(James 2:5)

Yet, even those who call ourselves Christians and affirm the divine authority of Scripture, read these verses then strive to be strong, first, and rich!

Since Enrique and I followed the Lord's call to a new place of ministry in Colonet, much has changed. The routine and order of the mission, our defined daily roles, and our savings account have all disappeared. After returning from the Philippines, Enrique settled into his new role as pastor while I stayed in San Diego, possibly setting a Guinness world record for "most car repairs done in a single month." I spent more time on Craig's List and in Home Depot than with human beings, and bought items that gave me no pleasure: plumbing, oven hood, master cylinder, toilet, ready-mix (which I'd never even heard of) and grout.

Enrique was thrilled when his wife called to say, "Whatever else we need can wait; I'm coming home!"

He went out and bought "sweet water" so his spoiled wife wouldn't have to shower in the salty water he'd been using all month.

"I spent fifty dollars, but that should last a month and we can cook with it!" he told me.

It was hard to act pleased, like we were getting Perrier delivered in grand quantities. Every day brought news of more things we needed but couldn't afford: doors, stove, shower, propane, furniture, labor - the list grew and with it, my anxiety and desperation.

"Where's your faith, Ellie?" my pastor husband asked me one day.

Where, indeed? It had shrunk to the size of my world, quite small. When the realization returned to me that my faith could win or lose spiritual battles, I decided to rejoin God's army. I stopped praying to Him as though He were my personal building contractor and asked instead for an attitude of trust and praise. I begged Him for deep love for the people of Jaramillo and Colonet. He responded with ministry and relationships.

In Sunday school, the children won my heart with their openness.

"Who wants prayer for someone in their family?" we asked.

More than half raised their hands with petitions for family members who were alcoholics or drug addicts. God gave Giovani, a young Bible School graduate, and me a passion to change these children's lives. Saturday we will begin a youth ministry using participatory-style lessons and activities to rock them into abundant godly lives.

The Lord began to gift me each day with opportunities that kept my mind off my material needs: a chance to minister to a young wife in crisis, early morning prayer meetings at the church, five worship services a week and feeling my adoption into the church family.

One night, climbing into bed, my husband brushing his teeth in the other room, I told him, "You know what, Enrique? This place feels more like home to me than anywhere I've ever lived!"

And one morning I awoke with no worries. Walking outside later carrying a bucket of laundry, heaven opened before me. The sun's warmth felt personal and perfect, a tree in the yard, perhaps not catching fire, still, glistened with the Presence of the Lord.

"I am on holy ground! The Lord is with me!"

This knowledge, so wonderful to me, did not leave me unchanged. Ordinary things became pleasurable. To have to fill the washing machine with a hose before the wash and rinse cycle made me glad. Not having a bathroom sink or shower became things I could look forward to. Our refrigerator, cars, health, began a long list of "haves" and the list of "have-nots" grew, if no shorter, less important. God showed me that the less one has materially, the easier it was to count one's blessings and recognize that every good gift came from above. Using the Lord's crazy math, I discovered I was rich!

One morning in my devotions, my mind kept returning to Enrique, how much he enjoyed serving the Lord and his generous love for me, so constant and faithful. Then my mind and heart went higher, seeing his affections as but a sample of God's abundant, unconditional, and eternal love. A song came to me, the truth of its lyrics carrying me into worship.

"And now, let the weak say 'I am strong,' let the poor say 'I am rich for what the Lord has done for us!"

Here, in our little unfinished home in Jaramillo, with the Lord, a godly husband, and great love for the people we serve, I can say with all my heart, "I'm rich!"

Christmas, 2010

Everyone has a favorite part of the Christmas story; some love the baby in a manger, others, the star that guided the wise men, or the tremendous faith of Mary and Joseph. What struck me most to wonder, though, was the angel of the Lord and a great heavenly host breaking heaven open for the shepherds. As a child I would study those cards which showed a piece of sky rolled back with heaven's brilliance shining down. The angels didn't matter to me; my heart's desire was to see what was up there, what was heaven like?

This yearning of my spirit dissolved on Christmas morning. My excitement of discovery descended from wondering about Heaven to opening my stocking and presents, a more immediate pleasure.

Fifty years later, all those gifts have long broken or been thrown away but I am still a child in the wonder of Heaven.

"Keep me in Your Presence, Lord! Don't let the cares of the day take me from You!"

This, a frequent prayer of mine, recognizes that Heaven is always open, and though I can't see the angels singing, I can reach it through prayer and obedience to Christ.

"The kingdom of God is near you," Jesus told us.

That knowledge fills me with the same awe, the same urgent desire to see heaven now.

"Thy kingdom come!"

Since our Lord Himself told us to pray in this manner my desire is not unattainable. But my life in this season is not one of wonders nor great works. We are in a stage of preparation for Community Health

Evangelism, an organized ministry of health and evangelism we hope to start in the spring. Our objective right now is "entering the community," getting to know the people we want to serve. Jesus gave supreme value to this "building of relationships;" yet, I've felt stagnant, like the real work was yet to begin.

Still, a man in the Bible received praise from Jesus when he said, *"To love (God) with all your heart, with all your understanding and with all your strength, and to love your neighbor as yourself is more important than all burnt offerings and sacrifices."* (Mark 12:33)

When Jesus heard him say this He told him what we all long to hear:

"You are not far from the kingdom of God."

Saturday night we opened the mission base to our congregants. Forty brothers- and sisters-in-Christ came. They brought roast turkey with stuffing, mashed potatoes and corn. I had dessert, a big carrot cake. In God's way, there was just enough and all was delicious. Then some men built a bonfire and, sitting in a huge circle, Enrique led us in worship while sparks shot up toward the starry sky.

"Do you want to hear my testimony?" Betty, a Bible School student asked.

She began but others followed, standing with their faces aglow behind the flames, giving glory to God for deliverance from drugs, alcohol, loneliness and sin.

"I am right where I'm supposed to be."

This assurance slipped into my consciousness and I offered it as thanksgiving to God. Looking around the circle I realized these simple folks had become both flock and friends.

"I love them," I realized, "and together, we'll seek God's abundant life."

In that circle, the flame in our center was Jesus, burning out differences. We were one.

God whispered, *"The kingdom of God is within you."*

And I peeked into an open heaven.

Wishing you and your family a Merry Christmas! May heaven open for you and let you "see" into the kingdom of God!

*With His love,
Ellie and Enrique*

2011

January 11, 2011

Enrique is a man of great passions. The more destructive of these have caused him problems, but that's a story for another day. By the time we met, the Holy Spirit had control of his limbic system. The third person of the Trinity had reined in the uglies but nurtured a keen sensitivity and enjoyment of life.

This morning my husband ran into the house like an excited child.

"Ellie, I just heard the most beautiful song! Come listen to it! To be honest, the words made me cry!"

His eyes watered a little just at the mention of it. I followed him to our truck where he turned up the volume on the CD player. Jesus Adrian Romero sang in Spanish and Enrique translated to be sure I understood.

"When no one is watching me,
in the intimate place where I can't say anything but the truth
Where there are no appearances,
Where my heart lies uncovered
There, I am sincere.
There, my appearance of piety leaves.
There, Your grace is all that matters.
Your forgiveness is what keeps me standing,
And I couldn't hold my head up if I were not redressed
in the grace and righteousness of the Lord.
It's Your grace and Your forgiveness that allows us to be called instruments of Your love."

The lyrics sounded much better in Spanish but the message was clear. The song described that delightful stripping away of pride, reputation, and sin, which leaves a person alone with God and grace. It was lovely, but there was no musician I preferred over my husband, no heart that sang more authentically to the Lord than his.

"Learn it! I want to hear you sing it!" I told him.

We don't have a music system in our house, so when I heard the song again a little later, I looked outside. Enrique was standing next to the truck with his guitar. As he listened to the original artist, he sought out the right chords and notes and sang along. I doubt he felt the sun on his back or realized the intensity on his face. What I saw was "serious enjoyment" and a desire to make this song his own. After an hour of practice he could harmonize perfectly with the CD, a little longer and he'd sing it in church.

He still cries at the lyrics, tears that come from having journeyed to that intimate place. They come from having had his reputation and piety stripped away, and from having sat alone with only God and His grace.

Is there anything better in marriage than watching your spouse worship God with all his heart?

"And I will give thanks to Him in song." Psalm 28:7

Tales of A Five-Star Missionary

Tales of A Five-Star Missionary

January 28, 2011

Yesterday some very important people visited our base: the children from FFHM's Day Home for Disabled Children.

Mary helped me decide the menu, something the kids could manage: chicken tacos with salsa and beans. I twisted a mountain of balloons into hearts, giraffes, and other animals and tied them to bushes and telephone poles, marking the road from the highway. Neighborhood children had appropriated most of them by the time my guests arrived, but nothing could destroy our excitement of being together. As the wheelchair-bound kids were lowered from the bus on a special ramp, others who could, ran to me. Their hugs and kisses were like medicine I didn't know I needed.

"Welcome kids! I'm so happy you're here!"

"Kiki?" they asked.

"Enrique's not here but he promised he'd get here as fast as he could!"

We served lunch and mingled. The older kids shocked me with how much English they'd learned from Ken, one of their teachers. Rosita, Domitila, Irma, Maria, and Zaida took turns telling me something in English and I gave them well-deserved praise.

"Ellie," Mary whispered, "do you think we could show the older girls inside your house?"

"Of course!" I answered. "But how will they get up the stairs?"

"The men will lift them in their chairs."

So, one by one, the guys hoisted the girls, a few, quite overweight, up the two steps into my kitchen. Sergio was one of those who had run to help. This handsome young man had been electrocuted at age fourteen by a downed high-tension wire. As a consequence, both legs had been amputated below the knees. To see him standing there, balanced on prosthetics and lifting the other handicapped filled me with an understanding of greatness.

The girls loved our little house and I tried to find things to make the tour more interesting.

"This is my personal Bible verse!" I told them, pointing to a frame over the stove. "Remember Chelsea, Edgardo's wife? She made this for me!"

It had a beautiful design next to the written Scripture. I gave a short testimony explaining the significance of the quote from Isaiah, then told them,

"You girls should choose your own Bible verse! Ask God to show you something He wants to say especially to you!"

"I have one," said Domi quietly.

This beautiful girl, paralyzed from the waist, was gifted with a nurturing undefeatable spirit.

"Mary read it to me once," she continued.

The site was Jeremiah 29:11, so I got a Bible and she read:

"For I know the plans I have for you," declares the Lord, "plans to prosper you and not to harm you, plans to give you a hope and a future."

With no means of mobility, this little girl used to sit on the cement floor of their house all day long while her mother worked. Now, she not only had her own wheelchair, but was attending public school with a dream of becoming a teacher. Jeremiah 29:11 was perfect for her.

We sang Happy Birthday, blew bubbles and opened presents. Javier received a watch.

"We gave all the boys watches for Christmas," Mary told me, "but I didn't get him one because he can't tell time! He asked me where was his? I felt so bad to have left him out, so I told him we'd give it to him on his birthday!"

It was difficult to believe this skeletal boy was now sixteen. His body was the weakest of all and he suffered teenage emotions with a child's intelligence. But clearly, the teenager was proud of his new watch. Dirk strapped it on his wrist, outside the shirtsleeve to pad it and keep it from turning, and Javier used all his strength to lift his arm and show everyone. We knew then, the only time that mattered was this precise moment.

The final event was a game. Sitting in a circle, the children passed around a rock while Enrique played music. Whoever held it when the music stopped was eliminated. For kids with Muscular Dystrophy, the task would have been impossible, so Sergio and Dirk helped the weak ones grab and pass the stone. With their aid, Javier, the weakest child, won. Dirk lifted the champion's bony arms in triumph but the kids barely noticed. This tight-knit group relished the camaraderie more than the competition; who won was not important.

What we ate, played, or said yesterday, wasn't important either; all that mattered was our love. How many times throughout the day did I give or receive a huge hug? How often did I look at a child and tell him or her, "I love you!" or "I missed you!"

Later, in the quiet, the Lord showed me what it all meant. In His light, we're all handicapped and we are all deeply loved. And sometimes, despite our own weaknesses, we help others to overcome theirs. Then we realize that God is with us and everyone who calls on Him, wins.

"Be imitators of God, therefore, as dearly loved children..."
(Eph. 5:1)

Ready for Games

Bryan and Angel with Enrique

Tales of A Five-Star Missionary

The Gang

January 30, 2011
"Call to me and I will answer you and show you great and unsearchable things that you do not know."
(Jeremiah 33:3)

What an astounding offer! God desires to reveal Himself and His wisdom, His hidden riches, to those who cry out. James encourages us to take advantage of the Lord's generosity, *"You do not have because you do not ask God."* (verse 4:2)

Recently these verses struck me with their incomparably great power. So, I began to pray daily for revelation - and God was faithful. His love, His presence, His protection surrounded me in my silent time and made me beg for more. During a morning jog, He spoke more precisely.

"Do battle for the oppressed in prayer!"

God had burdened my heart with the plight of the indigenous people. A recent visit to a camp where farm workers lived reignited my fury against the ranching system. The exploitation burdened laborers with meager wages, unsuitable housing, poor education and healthcare. Animals lived in better conditions.

The trail I ran on this morning wove between huge fields, some overgrown, some plowed and ready for planting. The only structure in sight was once a small white house, now crumbled into rocks and dirt, just one wall still intact. Not ten feet away stood a lovely tree, shaped perfectly with full green leaves, a proclamation of life. The two forms were all that rose above the vast flatness of the fields. They reminded me that all people are dwellings, inhabited by either a spirit of life or of death. Many are in decay like this house, oblivious to the tree of life so nearby!

Fueled by fresh revelation, I began to do spiritual battle for the Indian workers.

"May they know truth, Lord, so they will not believe the lies the ranchers tell them: that these conditions are acceptable! May they put on shields of faith and extinguish all the fiery darts the evil one uses to keep them oppressed, and may we carry the gospel of peace to them!"

Later that day, I related this all in church. Much of the congregation worked in the fields so when I spoke about "unfair wages" and "the unjust ranching system" they shouted out some strong "Amens!" However, as usual whenever I thought I had it all figured out, God showed me I didn't.

Pastor Mayito struggled to a standing position, leaning to one side to relieve his arthritic hip. He was a man of the land; he'd worked for ranchers and been a rancher. He'd raised cows and goats and grown or picked every native crop. Only late in life had he become a pastor after God miraculously healed him of liver disease and alcoholism.

"Hermanos," he began, "I have something to say! You're right that things need changing! The Indians who work the farms *are* in darkness! But they *chose* it! They've heard the gospel many times and don't want any part of it! Missionaries and church groups have gone out and presented Jesus to them but no, they rejected Him! They practice witchcraft and worship idols. So God removed His blessing from the land! I remember years ago, there used to be jobs for everyone. Eight thousand hectares (1 hectare = 2.47 acres) were producing in abundance; now, not even one thousand! So many people don't have work, but let's not blame it all on the ranchers! God says in 2 Chronicles 7:14, *"If my people, who are called by my name, will humble themselves and pray and seek my face and turn from their wicked ways, then I will hear from heaven and will forgive their sin and will heal their land."*

I listened in silence. This was a man of great compassion, an evangelist. He was not saying, "Forget about them; they're lost!" But he was clarifying that the people's hard hearts had brought about consequences.

In the end, the information served to reinforce the revelation God had given. This is a battle which can only be won in the Lord's power. We are fighting generations of strongholds, but the victory will be ours, and theirs. They need transformational ministry like "Community Health Evangelism," to teach them truth, so *they* can dispel the lies that have enslaved them! They need to see the power of the gospel so they will long to make it their own, and finally, they need to find their dignity in Christ so they will then choose His righteousness.

Victory will not come through endless donations of used clothes. It will come through persistent, faith-filled, aggressive prayer and a manner of ministry that empowers the poor and restores hope.

Bill Johnson, in his book The *Supernatural Power of a Transformed Mind,* says this about revelation: "You'll know when He (God) is speaking because it will have a freshness to it. It will always be better than anything you could have thought up yourself. And if He gives you new ideas, they will probably be impossible for you to accomplish in your own strength."

The revelation He gave me met these criteria. Please join the battle through your prayers!

Tales of A Five-Star Missionary

Farmworkers' Housing

Tree of life

February 23, 2011

Concerning revelation, St. John of the Cross wrote, "For an adequate exposition of this subject, God would have to move my hand and pen."

What happened Sunday at Enrique's ordination was also beyond human faculties. The best I can say is a body of believers, united by one Holy Spirit, rejoiced in the treasures of knowing their Lord Jesus, and the love of God flowed from one to another as freely as the Baja wind.

Unity and service made the event possible. People from three churches provided for the banquet. Those who could gave fifty or a hundred pesos; those who couldn't gave a kilo of beans, rice, tortillas. For the main course, *birria*, a type of stew, Pastor Mayito bought unblemished organically-raised beef from his friend. The harmony shown by women from three different congregations sharing one kitchen could only have come from God.

"You two are an answer to prayer!" Pastor Dennis told Enrique and me.

Dennis McNally and a team from New Life Christian Church in Castro Valley, California, built the mission base we now occupy.

"We always wanted a bilingual couple with giftings like yours," he said.

No sense of pride could result from the statement, just a deep gratefulness to God for the blessing of our call. As the Senior Presbyter of "Life Links International," Dennis travels internationally, blessing pastors and missionaries with prophetic directions and apostolic oversight. He had come with three other men, George and Tim, who also prophesy, and Gonzalo, their interpreter. They kept thanking us for our hospitality but to Enrique and me, it was like having our parents thank us for not making them stay in a hotel.

After days of fierce rain, Sunday lived up to its name. We stood outside the small church in Jaramillo greeting our guests. Many had come from the orphanage, intimate friends who understood the long road that had led to this day. And so many pastors! I longed for spiritual eyes as these servants of God entered the church, God's chosen instruments in my husband's life: from Tijuana, Ensenada, the Bible Institute, the mission, Pastor Avitia, who married us, and Mayito, Enrique's pastor and mentor now.

"The Holy Spirit is here! Let's sing praise to God!"

We sang as we ought, with overwhelming gratitude and the assurance that every good gift was from above.

"I haven't been this excited since my wedding day!" I told people around me.

In Mexico, they often ordain pastors together with their wives. I had declined, believing the Biblical training and spiritual formation Enrique completed did not automatically transfer to me. However, after ordaining him, Pastor Dennis, George, and Tim took turns prophesying over us as a couple.

Now the Holy Spirit set the church on fire! Now Dennis' anointing was clear. We knew it was not men from Castro Valley speaking, but God. I will not diminish the revelation by attempting to retell it. God will remind us of the words at the proper time but what remained in us was great joy and an unquenchable desire to love. To quote St. John of the Cross again, revelations which impart knowledge of God to a soul, "produce an incomparable delight; there are no words or terms to describe them, for they occasion knowledge and delight of God Himself, and as David says: *"there is nothing like unto Him."* (Ps. 39:6)

So it was. The prophets left us with specific words which encouraged us and may guide us in the future. The real message, though, was contemplative, a sweet touch from God, impossible to express. It came not only from the prophets' mouths but from the one heart, the one love that joined all present. It made us want only to please Him, to do whatever He asked, because His love is everything.

> *"O daughters of Jerusalem, I charge you-*
> *if you find my lover,*
> *what will you tell him?*
> *Tell him I am faint with love."*
> (Song of Sol. 5:8)

My Husband, A Happy Man

March 30, 2011

One of my favorite writers, Anne Lamott, said there are only two kinds of prayer: "Help me, help me, help me!" and "Thank you, thank you, thank you!"

In this season of my life, when the "Help me's!" alone could fill my days, I find a third manner is necessary – the prayer of silence. To rest in God's presence and let all thoughts and desires float down the surface of a river while I sit far below, submerged in His Holiness. It is a prayer of faith because in His Presence, one recognizes there is nothing that needs to be said nor a thought worth thinking. We can leave everything to Him who is completely trustworthy.

This is not to say I don't begin with all kinds of concerns and petitions:

"How can I meet and find favor among the leaders of Colonet?"

"How can I present "Community Health Evangelism" to them in a way that will make it most desirable?"

"What kinds of livelihood training can we provide?"

"Lord, make this ministry more than health education; make it a means to bring whole communities to abundant life in Christ!"

My list is long, including both general and specific needs of our friends and families, our health, financial support, issues within the three churches we pastor, plus global concerns. On Fridays, Enrique and I spend hours together in verbal prayer for all these. However, my requests evaporate during "Centering Prayer," an appropriate name for a practice which brings the deepest part of our being to the Center of all that is. Here, I know that He knows all my concerns and longings, so I cast all my cares on Him and let Him care for me. Soon enough, my loftiest petitions seem petty; I only want His will to be done, in me and over all the earth. Now, I love Him enough to hallow His name and recognize He is my daily bread, all I need for life and life abundant.

Basil Pennington, in his book simply titled, *Centering Prayer,* quotes our Lord's great offer from Revelation, "Look, I am standing at the door, knocking." He tells us, "Centering Prayer is but a simple way to open the door – wide - all the way - to let Him come in."

Once we are with Him in this way, we'll want to remain. Pennington later compares a moment of contemplation of our Lord to Peter's ecstasy at seeing the transfiguration of Jesus.

He writes, "This experience of God at the center of our being also creates in us a desire to stay there enjoying the holy and wholly satisfying presence: *"Lord, it is good for us to be here. Let us build tents."*

I love the way Psalm 63:2-3 describes the experience: *"I have seen You in the sanctuary and beheld Your power and glory. Because Your love is better than life, my lips will glorify You."*

Even with moments of great communion, I've struggled with this time of waiting. Though the past months have been crucial in building relationships within the community we want to serve, the "Martha" in me has wanted to rush out and "do" more. Yet, the story of Mary, anointing the feet of Jesus with costly perfume, brings me perspective and joy.

Father Pennington compares our prayer time with the precious ointment. "What extravagance! With Judas, something in us cries: What waste! And yet she is not only defended by the Master, she is praised and exalted... Yes, the poor will always be there, the scandal of the poor, and they will need to be ministered to, but there will also be the scandal of the waste of lives poured out in homage...As we sit quietly with the Lord and pour out upon Him one of our most precious possessions, our time and the flow of our life, something within us cries: "Why this waste! This time could be spent in serving the terrible needs of the poor!...But what our Lord is proclaiming here is that He does want us to pour out ourselves on Him personally, to no apparent profit, even to the apparent detriment of His beloved poor."

So I come more often to sit with Him, sensing my utter unworthiness to call Him, "Father" yet knowing that as my Father, He will meet all my needs, all of Colonet's needs and those of all the earth. When I rise from these sessions, I sense that I have prayed for everyone on my list though I've not uttered a single word.

Now I am ready to come down from the mountain and meet the waiting crowds and problems. But, having prayed with faith, I expect what Father Thomas Keating, another Trappist monk and leader of the Centering Prayer movement writes, "The union that one discovers in contemplative prayer will not be reserved to that time. Moments of silence will overtake you in the course of daily life. Reality will tend to become more transparent. Its divine Source will shine through it."

In that state, everything is ministry and fruit, whether I am counseling, teaching, or hanging clothes on the line to dry. We don't need to build tents as Peter wanted to enjoy the divine presence of Christ; we *are* His tents!

"Remain in me, and I will remain in you. No branch can bear fruit by itself; it must remain in the vine. Neither can you bear fruit unless you remain in me."
(John 15:4)

April 6, 2011

Enrique has become, without knowing it, the Community Health Evangelism champion for Colonet, Mexico. He preaches to our three congregations concerning the strongholds of poverty and disease versus the power we have in Christ to be free.

"Do you think Jesus died so we can live in despair, always hungry, sick, out of work, addicted to drugs and alcohol? No! These are tools Satan uses to keep people oppressed! Christ came to open our eyes, to see the truth - poverty is not the inheritance of the children of God! He wants us to be healthy in body, mind and spirit; to have abundant life!"

I would not have believed this was the same man who was with me during last summer's "CHE" residency. How he had struggled those two long months in the Philippines! Muggy heat and plugged infected ears made it all the more difficult to learn in English, his second language, and spoken with various Asian accents! The real problem, though, stemmed from not being sure what CHE had to do with him as a pastor.

"I support you one hundred percent, Ellie! You can be the CHE leader and base it in our church, but why do I need to learn about worms?"

With God's usual timing, which is perfect but often seems late, Enrique's enlightenment came during our last week of training. Reverend Terry Darwymple, spoke about CHE in Enrique's favorite language, the word of God.

"CHE is based on Isaiah 61:1-4," he told us.

The day's class had finished, but the Holy Spirit had hold of Terry.

"Poverty, filthy living, hopelessness, and addictions keep people oppressed! Community Health Evangelism attacks physical, emotional and spiritual strongholds - Satan's tools. Through holistic health education and the Gospel, people's lives and entire communities are empowered and transformed. Once they raise their heads above their suffering, they can find answers to their problems and the first answer is Christ!"

He spoke at length about the spiritual aspect of CHE. Enrique listened spellbound. His eyes filled with tears as the Holy Spirit guided him into biblical truth. He looked at me and mouthed a big, "Wow!" Everything changed for him in that hour.

"Pastors need to know this!" he said.

I restrained from telling him, "No kidding!"

For his final project due the next day, Enrique wrote a CHE lesson that taught pastors the connection between CHE and the Gospel.

We are now in the "Entering the Community" phase of ministry in Punta Colonet, Baja California, Mexico. I have done an awareness seminar with church members, but my husband's sermons, sprinkled with insights from the Bible relating to health of body, mind and soul are pearls, leading our congregation on a path toward CHE.

April 18, 2011

The Gardener is at work, pruning, pruning, until the vine is bare. At least that's my perspective. Every sign of fruit, every leaf has been taken from me. CHE is on hold until I can present it to the Religious Association next month and even then, we need to find a site that has hope of success in a land of dependency. My health has been clipped so far down that I can't work. Even reading and praying feel like empty labor performed by an unclear mind and a dry heart.

I don't feel like a wife, just a burden, though my dear husband shows no less devotion.

"Why am I here, Lord? In this geographical, emotional, spiritual and circumstantial location? Would you please give me a hint, some morsel of revelation, so I can feel like a missionary again, a Christian, Your child?"

No response. Yet there, over my stove, the calligraphic framed words of Isaiah, a long-dead prophet, speak to me:

"I took you from the ends of the earth,
From its furthest corners I called you.
I said, "You are my servant,
I have chosen you and not rejected you.
So do not fear, for I am with you;
do not dismay, for I am your God.
I will strengthen you and help you
and raise you up with my righteous right hand."

Years ago, when I was in the basement of my life emotionally, the Lord used these bible verses to show me once and forever that I was His. Looking at the words now erase my need to understand. My circumstances are what He thinks best for me. It even gives me a bizarre sort of pleasure at seeing no purpose or fruit in my life.

"The only thing that counts is faith acting itself out in love." (Gal. 5:6)

I'm His. He is always with me, helping me, and sooner or later, in His perfect timing, He will raise me up.

May 1, 2011

Enrique is light in the Lord, but he entered the darkness of Tijuana and came back with our stolen truck.

"I know these people," he told me.

If this were supposed to reassure me, it failed. Still, he had spent a chunk of his life in darkness and becoming Christian had not erased his street savvy. So a few hours after we discovered the theft, my husband connected with people he'd not spoken to in years.

"I don't want to know who did it; I'm not going to the police. I just want my truck back!"

He said this to a man he later identified the as one of twenty in the immediate area who bought and sold stolen cars.

"Such a fine city!" I remarked.

The idea of having to buy back our own truck infuriated me, but the alternative was to lose it forever.

At eleven-thirty that night, the dealer, Joe, called Enrique.

"They offered me your truck, a 2004 GMC Sierra. There's a bible in it, so it must be yours!"

His "friends" had been amazed at the change in my husband and he had freely given the credit to Jesus. But when he left to meet with these thieves in the middle of the night I sat up and began to pray. Three hours later, he called.

"I'm okay; I'm with people I know, and we're negotiating."

Angry, worried, and totally dependent on God, I prayed nonstop till Enrique returned to his mother's house at four a.m.

"Tomorrow we'll get the truck," he said. "Now let's go to sleep."

So, after myriad phone calls and bargaining, we ended up paying four hundred dollars ransom for our pickup!

"You know everyone involved!" I said. "Why don't you just go to the police?"

"Believe me, I thought of it! I have all the names, but it would put my mother in danger. She asked me not to!"

"Just pay the scoundrels and let it go!" she ordered.

"Such evil!" I exclaimed.

"Yes, but I gave my testimony to a bunch of them!" Enrique said, smiling.

"How did they respond?"

"They respected me! Joe shook my hand and said, 'That's great, brother! Good for you! I'm glad one of us made it out!"

"Weird!" my comment. "Well, who knows how God will work?"

"Exactly!"

A few days later, the Lord completely restored my health after a month-long kidney infection. I received the truck and the healing as what they were – gifts from God. I don't pretend to understand it all; I hated being sick for so long and I hated paying evil men for our own vehicle, but the trial gave me perspective.

Health is more important than cars or money and a right relationship with God, more important than life. In glory, I may ask Jesus to explain this past month to me, but God Himself walked with me - consoling, teaching, loving and finally, restoring me, and I love Him more than ever. For new awareness of how utterly dependent I am on Him for any good thing and for the revelation of His transformational love, I exalt His holy name!

"Praise the Lord, O my soul;

all my inmost being, praise His holy name.
Praise the Lord, O my soul,
And forget not all His benefits –
Who forgives all your sins
And heals all your diseases,
Who redeems your life from the pit
And crowns you with love and compassion,
Who satisfies your desires with good things
So that your youth is renewed like the eagle's."
(Psalm 103:1-5)

May 31, 2011

C.S. Lewis once wrote, "Faith is telling your emotions where to get off!"

I thank God that reality is not based on my roller coaster of emotions. Every time we obtained a letter of recommendation for Enrique's visa or a written invitation to preach, lead worship, attend a conference in the U.S., my heart and confidence soared. Sunday in church we held hands and a man led us in prayer for various concerns. When he said, "Lord, arrange all the documents and open the way for Enrique's visa," I felt something like a soft breeze blow through my body, head to toe, leaving an unmistakable peace.

"The Lord gave me peace!" I told Enrique when he called from Tijuana. "I know they're going to approve you!"

"Everyone's telling me that," he responded.

The appointment was at seven am. I called his cell phone every half hour starting at seven-thirty but got voicemail.

"Call me as soon as you know!" I recorded.

At nine o'clock I was in a meeting at the mission clinic. Marisol, from the office, saw me and told me, "Ellie! Your husband was just trying to call you!"

"Oh! Great! Did he say anything about his visa?"

Poor Marisol! She tightened every muscle in her sweet face trying to restrain her bad news but it escaped through her eyes.

"What! He didn't get it? I don't believe it!"

There were too many friends in the clinic. I couldn't bear that much compassion, especially from Christians who would encourage me in the faith. Running outside for air, I asked the Lord, "Why did you give me such a strong sense of peace?"

He used my friend, Dirk, to answer me.

"Maybe He was telling you to have peace no matter what," he suggested.

"Why did you have to say that, Dirk? That's the right answer, you creep!"

The Lord has a ways to go before I "tell my emotions where to get off" in every difficult moment, but I'm progressing. In short order, my feelings began to fall in line with the truth. God had known I would need His special touch so He had encouraged me to have peace, and surprisingly, I did! Just half an hour later, I went to the cafeteria to have lunch with my favorite friends, the special needs children.

Mary, the program director and my special friend told me, "I'm so sorry you didn't get the visa! The kids prayed for Enrique this morning!"

Many of the children were listening to our conversation. Rosita, always tender, gave me a look of such sad compassion it jolted me into right thinking.

"Oh, Lord!" I thought. "They need to know that You heard them!"

So, embracing two of the older girls, I told them all, "Thanks, you guys, for praying! Don't think God didn't listen; He did! He just has a better plan that we don't know about."

Their faith was that of children, strong and not easily shaken. They turned peacefully back to their meatball soup and I turned back to God. My emotions bowed to His peace.

"As the heavens are higher than the earth,
so are my ways higher than your ways
and my thoughts than your thoughts…"
(Isaiah 55:9)

June 7, 2011

Our precious Javier should not be alive. He's emaciated; takes only sips of liquids, and can't cough hard enough to expel the secretions that block his airways. He has end stage Muscular Dystrophy and without a hint of fear, tells us with an upwards nod of his head, that he's ready to be with Jesus!

Those of us who love him are ready to release him from suffering. We've watched him get weaker and weaker, been amazed as he survived one pneumonia after another, twice at the threshold of death. God is perfecting this son through suffering and few believers exhibit the likeness of Christ as does this faith-filled adolescent.

"He is such a joy!" Mary remarked. "But it's getting so difficult for him!"

She and her husband, Dirk, have cared for him since his release from the hospital, per family request. Day and night they turn him, hold him prone while secretions drain out of his mouth, offer him liquids, pray. The boy rewards them with one blessing after another, an unexpected joke, a loud "Amen!" after every prayer, or just his peace that surpasses all understanding.

When I visited on Saturday, Javier was having a rough time. He had had a coughing spell that exhausted him, severe body aches, and did not want to be on the couch. Mary had washed the bed sheets and hung them to dry so Javier had to stay in the living room. He didn't like it.

"Solo treinta minutos!" she told him with her wonderful Dutch-accented Spanish.

Every few minutes he opened his eyes and spoke as loudly as his frail lungs would allow, *"Cama!"*

He was telling us he wanted to go back to bed, but even in his discomfort there was no teenage rebelliousness to his voice. The gentleness and respect with which he made his desire known was like Christ's "*I thirst!*"

"Want me to massage your foot, Javier?" I asked.

"Si!"

He didn't like to be touched now; everything hurt. Yet he never tired of having his feet gently stroked. So I took his left foot in my hands and began to rub the bottom with my palm. Soon he quieted and fell asleep but I never stopped, partly not wanting him to wake up and find that I'd failed him, but more, because it was like rubbing the foot of Jesus on the Cross. It was pale, elegant, contracted downward, with even a scab on the ankle like a tiny stigmata. I rubbed it toes to heel, over and over, until time disappeared. What pleasure to have some means of comforting him, Christ, even all who suffered! It was prayer.

Yesterday Enrique and I visited him together. Javier loved Enrique's worship so he brought his guitar.

"Do you want Kiki to sing?" I asked.

"Si," he answered without hesitation.

My husband began in his wonderful way to lead us into the presence of God through song. Javier's eyes were closed but he followed along, so softly, that at times we could not hear him, only see his lips move. Then on certain lyrics, his favorites, he'd open his eyes and with concentrated effort, sing certain praises out loud.

"*Vamos a cantar con la música del cielo!*" (We will sing the music of heaven!)

He could only sing a few syllables so it sounded like, *muse celo,* but it came from a heart so close to God, the holiness made us cry.

"*How beautiful you are and how pleasing!*" we knew God was saying to His special son. (Song of Sol. 7:6)

Javier's worship was a perfectly-aged drink offered to the divine palate.

"May the wine go straight to my lover, flowing gently over lips and teeth."
(Song of Sol. 7:9)

The Lord drank and was pleased.

Ellie, Javier, and Enrique

June 13, 2011

Our best evidence shows us that eighty percent of premature heart disease, eighty percent of strokes and diabetes, as well as forty percent of cancer can be prevented by appropriate diet and exercise and not smoking. Yet, many people settle for taking medicine for the rest of their lives, even with the risk of harmful side effects, rather than eat correctly, exercise, and feel better.

Jesus asked the man by the pool, an invalid for thirty-eight years, "Do you want to get well?"

Saturday we asked the same question to those who attended a holistic health fair at our church in Colonet. We measured each person and figured out his or her Body Mass Index, the most accurate way to assess if someone is underweight, normal, overweight, or obese. While they waited to see one of the doctors, a nurse taught them what an appropriate diet is. I had hesitated before delegating this important teaching station, thinking to do it myself. In the end I deferred to the "Community Health Evangelism" practice of utilizing local people whenever possible. Alma, the nurse I chose, has lived here her whole life. She taught the material expertly, much better than I could have, fine-tuning it to the local food and culture.

When it was time for their consultation, the doctor took the patient's blood pressure. One reason for this was that the Joint National Committee on High Blood Pressure recommends that "persons should be seated quietly for at least 5 minutes in a chair (rather than on an exam table), with feet on the floor, and arm supported at heart level. Our doctors could proceed with their health questions and education for more than five minutes before taking the blood pressure. The second reason was that since we were not giving out any medicine, people could still feel the doctor "did something."

However, the real work of our physicians, or any health practitioner, was to determine which patients were at risk for serious disease through lifestyle choices, high blood pressure, elevated Body Mass Index (BMI), and counsel them. Statistically, people are more apt to obey if it is a doctor who tells them they need to quit smoking, lose weight, or change their diet. However, in today's rushed schedule, it takes much less time to prescribe a med than to work with someone on diet, stress management, and an exercise program.

"Do you want to get well?" is what we were really asking.

Although I had pre-judged them, thinking they would just leave disappointed that they hadn't received any drugs, in reality, many said, "Yes!" They wanted to be healthy! They wanted to learn more about diet and exercise, how to prevent diseases like Diabetes, which, to me, is statistically high in Mexico, but to them, is what's harming or killing their brother, mother, uncle, friend.

God is good. One of the subjects I'm most passionate about – diet and exercise – is what my flock wants to learn! So we are going to start a group at the church and once a week we will walk together, study, and pray. God created us body, mind and soul. Hopefully we will bless all three through this group!

Alma Teaching

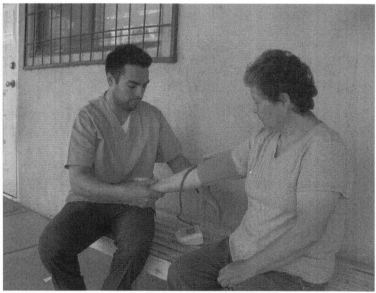

Dr. Heber Taking Blood Pressure

June 15, 2011

"Samaritan woman: 33 year old female found to have high blood pressure (150/90), gastro-esophageal reflux disease, chronic depression, migraine headaches, and chronic right shoulder pain.

Treated with: Enalapril 10 mg daily and Hydrochlorothiazide 25 mg once a day for the hypertension, Prozac 20 mg daily for depression, Ibuprofen 400 mg every 4-6 hours as needed for shoulder pain or mild headache, Relpax 40 mg as needed for migraine headache. Oh! And the little purple pill for her heartburn!"

That's how the woman at the well might have been diagnosed and treated had she met a short-term medical mission team instead of Jesus Christ. The visiting doctor – a stranger with a long line of patients waiting to be seen – would not likely have acquired an in-depth history, so he couldn't have taken into account the traumas and stressors underlying the woman's symptoms.

Jesus, the perfect holistic healer, knew:

1. The Samaritan woman had had four marriages, ending through divorce, death or abandonment, leaving her with unresolved complicated grief, loss of hope and a hard heart.
2. She was now living outside of wedlock, causing her emotional insecurity, diminished self-esteem and social ostracism.
3. Her neighbors and community alternatively shunned and mocked her. She responded to this ongoing stress and abuse with bouts of anger and depression.

"You are a Jew and I am a Samaritan woman. How can you ask me for a drink?"

She met Christ's simple request for water with misplaced sarcasm and resentment. Yet, he responded with divine patience in words she didn't understand but which somehow birthed in her hope long dead.

"If you knew the gift of God and who it is who asks you for a drink, you would have asked him and he would have given you living water."

Now her edge was gone. She called him, *"Sir."*

He continued to woo her soul through his gentleness and respect. How long since she had been treated so kindly? She admitted her thirst; indeed her soul was parched.

"Sir, give me this water..."

But Christ always heals holistically. He knew she could not tolerate his living water until her ulcerous palate was healed of sin. So he brought her deeds into his Light, not to condemn her but to laser away her emotional scars, her confession meeting his forgiveness and love.

She was not used to such honesty. She called him a *"prophet"* then changed the subject. Again, he respected her, switching to the new topic yet using it to lead her deeper into truth.

"Believe me, woman, a time is coming when you will worship the Father..."

She didn't know the Father, yet standing here talking with this amazing man, she felt like she did. And as she made the connection between the one who made her feel whole and the Messiah, Jesus revealed himself to her.

"I who speak to you am he."

Forgiven, respected, loved. Now she was ready to forgive and love others. She had hope and purpose, a passionate evangelist with no time for self-pity. All she could think of was bringing others to Christ.

Jesus healed her mind and soul and in so doing, prevented all the physical repercussions of stress. Without drugs.

So Dr. Heber, at our health fair Saturday, sent a woman complaining of headaches for counsel and prayer. She had a good marriage and four healthy children but worried all the time about money. She had accepted Jesus once but never really followed him.

"He cares about you and your family, your finances, everything! Let Him be your Father!" I urged her.

We asked her questions, shared the word of God, listened and prayed.

During our session, I watched the muscles in her face relax. She left with a new expression - hope, even joy.

Much better than Motrin.

July 27, 2011

"Kiki, aquí!" Javier told me.

It meant he wanted Enrique to visit again and sing worship. I didn't think it were possible but Javier had gotten skinnier, truly now just skin on bones. Every position, every wrinkle, real or imagined, bothered him. So to have a means of bringing him pleasure was an honor. Enrique came the next day.

"What song do you want?" he asked.

"*Tu.*"

That meant, "You decide!"

My husband began to move in his gifting and the Holy Spirit transformed sadness into sweetness. Javier's eyes opened wide and he smiled a lot, at Mary, "Kiki," and me. I have spent thousands of dollars in my life seeking pleasure – adventures, fine restaurants, trips around the world; but to receive his smile, to share in his joy was – well, as the credit card ad says – priceless!

"*Alaba a Dios! Alaba a Dios!*" Enrique sang.

This song, not surprisingly one of Javier's favorites, encouraged us to praise God no matter what.

"*Estas llorando? Alaba! En la prueba, alaba! Estas sufriendo? Alaba! No importa, alaba! Tu alabanza El escuchará!*"

"Are you crying? Praise Him! In trials, praise Him! Are you suffering? Praise Him! No matter what, praise Him! God will hear your praise!"

A dying child, using all his puny strength to sing praise to the Lord – surely angels celebrated and the Father's heart broke with love.

On the way home Enrique said, *"Ya está en la plenitud!"*

This was one of those statements that was so much better in Spanish, but it signified, "He's already living in the fullness of Christ."

It was true. It was why everyone who visited Javier came away blessed. It was why Dirk and Mary, caring for him day and night for over a month, still felt it a privilege. And it's why Christ came – so we all may live in the "plenitude" of our Savior.

Little Javier showed us what it looked like.

"And I pray that you, being rooted and established in love, may have power, together with all the saints, to grasp how wide and long and high and deep is the love of Christ, and to know this love that surpasses knowledge – that you may be filled to the measure of all the fullness of God."
(Ephes. 3:17-19)

July 29, 2011

"Don't you miss your house?"

"Aren't you afraid of all the violence in Mexico?"

"Is it hard to go without the comforts we have in the U.S.?"

To these questions people ask me, my answer is "No, no, no!" However there is one thing I do miss, something I used to do regularly and enjoyed again on my last visit home. That was - to jog Moonlight Beach at low tide while conversing with God. He spoke so clearly sometimes I had to stop, lift up my arms, and praise Him! Then I'd sit in the sand and do Centering Prayer, silent before God with an open heart.

The first wave of His presence washed away my thoughts, as flimsy and ungrounded as sand castles. Then His glory swept over me as pure joy. Like the ocean, His kingdom was a world I could only enter completely by dying. Yet my longing to be with Him overcame all fear. In the stillness His Spirit could work; my will died and His became my one desire.

Yet, even as I rose, feeling such harmony, the world screamed for my attention and I turned. His presence receded, leaving only a film of glory, but I carried the ecstasy of immersion with me and hoped never to dry.

July 12, 2011

Javier is gone from our sight. He has gone to live in his mansion in heaven, the place God prepared for him. He took this boy of faith so that where Jesus is, Javier may be also. Of course, the youngster knew about it beforehand and was even a bit cocky regarding his reward.

"Mi casa!" Javier told Dirk one day.

They were about to watch a Disney movie and the fairytale castle came on the screen. Whatever Bible teaching the boy had received had stuck. He was telling Dirk, "There's my house!"

"Dónde?" Dirk asked him, *"Aquí?"* (*"Where? Here?"*)

"No," he replied, shaking his head.

Dirk guessed, "Camalu?" where Javier had lived with his family in poverty.

Wrong again.

"No."

"Dónde?"

Dirk already knew the answer. Javier jerked his head back and looked heavenward, explaining to his somewhat slow friend.

"Allá!" There!"

Then he added, *"Mas grande!"* Bigger!

I struggled before writing this. Javier was great and the word "eulogy" was derived from the Greek, meaning "high praise." It is an honor but also a huge challenge to capture his spirit and praise his life adequately. Crowds of witnesses who loved him can testify to this. He was simple, but not. His body grew weaker while his faith and his spirit strengthened and matured beyond understanding. He suffered all his sixteen years, yet constantly conquered his pain.

Not that he didn't hurt or feel sad. At my wedding, sitting next to my friend and his, Nora, he told her, "Ellie se casa." *Ellie's getting married.*

"Si," said Nora.

"Yo, nunca." Me, never.

Statements like this showed me - Javier realized he had been robbed of a normal life. I don't know what form his suffering took before knowing Christ. But the word of God entered his life over three years ago when Dave and Carrie Irving started a Bible study in the family's home. Javier and his brother, Feliciano, experienced the love of Christ poured out into their lives through missionaries at the orphanage, in the school for handicapped children, and they were baptized one cold Sunday in a tin tub.

Since that glorious day Javier, especially, had become the very word of God, Romans 5:4. His suffering produced perseverance. His body bore witness to the fact that sin and death had entered the world. Muscular Dystrophy was a genetic disease, inbred in humans just as sin. Yet the harder his body made him suffer, the greater the perseverance it produced. He lived the past year on some ethereal combination of will and grace, dominating death and holding it at bay. And what can we say about the sweet, joyous, gentle, wise, Christ-like character this perseverance produced? Only that everyone who surrounded him came away blessed. Visiting him, for me, became a healthy addiction. I craved what he had, what spilled out on me when I spent time with him. He had achieved the character that came from knowing Christ and sharing in His sufferings.

With that character came hope. Javier's hope certainly did not lie in anything financial or material, nor, at the end, for longer days, strong muscles, or even life, not at least, in this world. His hope lay in the very love God had poured out into his heart by the Holy Spirit,

Whom He had given to Javier. He rejoiced in the hope of the glory of God and that hope did not disappoint him.

At his memorial service, we saw his discarded tent, the physical body that had succumbed to death. But on an easel next to the casket, a photograph showed the Javier we knew – his smile that had the power to lift any heart and his eyes which shone with gentleness and great love. Never had I been so aware that a cadaver had nothing to do with the person. His face in the photograph shouted his triumph.

"Where, o death, is your victory?
"Where, o death, is your sting?"

It's lovely to think of him with Jesus, basking in His perfect love and joy, understanding all things were for his good. He has been perfected and reminds us, it is not what we do that matters, it is who we become.

Tales of A Five-Star Missionary

"Well done, good and faithful servant!"
(Matt.25:21)

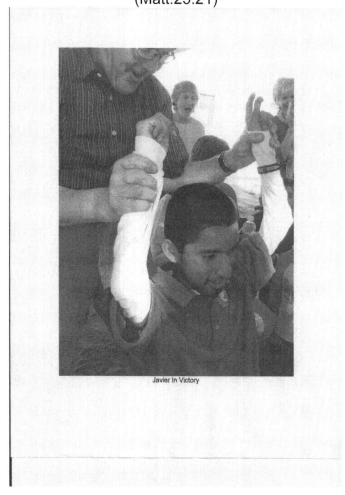

Javier In Victory

July 17, 2011

Feliciano's funeral was a déjà vu. Didn't we just meet together to mourn? Didn't we just see this white casket, the memorial flower sprays, an easel holding a photograph of the boy we loved?

Yet, the second service was harder, heavier, not because we loved Javier any less – certainly not – but because our human hearts had been bombarded with grief.

"I don't want to cry anymore," Maria told me.

She had raised the boys. Their grandmother, usually vigorous, walked slowly and stooped, as if the monumental burden she carried had actual physical weight.

Mary leaned over and asked me, "Did you see Galdino's shirt?"

The father of the children, sat erect, with no expression, receiving our hugs and condolences woodenly. No external cracks showed in his armor, but what he had chosen to put on today, a certain long-sleeved T-shirt, spoke to all who knew. His eldest son had loved the excitement of the paramedics and fire ministry at the mission. A few times they had taken Javier for a ride, let him sit in the driver's seat, and wear a helmet. When they gave him his own "Bombero" T-shirt, he wore it proudly, one of the team. Now his Dad wore it, honoring one son while burying another.

"It's too much!" many said.

It felt that way. Especially when the boys' half-brother, who also has Muscular Dystrophy, was wheeled forward by his father. Little Jose held out a toy bus and looked up at Dirk, who stood ceremonially next to the coffin. Dirk lifted the glass cover and Jose dropped in his parting gift for his friend.

Sweet Feliciano! A true child who craved mothering. He lacked the victorious spirit of his older brother, yet, he too, had a great capacity to love and flourished when he was loved back. Both boys were in heaven and in spite of all the sadness, we believed.

"Faith is telling your emotions where to get off," wrote C. S. Lewis.

Never were those words more applicable! When Dirk closed with the following verses from Revelation, their utter truth lifted me.

> *"Then I saw a new heaven and a new earth, for the first heaven and the first earth had passed away, and there was no longer any sea. I saw the Holy City, the new Jerusalem, coming down out of heaven from God, prepared as a bride beautifully dressed for her husband. And I heard a loud voice from the throne saying, "Now the dwelling of God is with men, and he will live with them. They will be his people, and God himself will be with them and be their God. He will wipe every tear from their eyes. There will be no more death or mourning or crying or pain, for the old order of things has passed away. He who was seated on the throne said, "I am making everything new!" ...He who overcomes will inherit all this, and I will be his God and he will be my son." (Rev. 21:1-4, 7)*

These words, from God's own mouth, refocused me. When the tragedy of the fallen world steals joy, when Satan would have us look on the casket and the cross rather than the resurrection, then we must assert our faith. We must deliberately fix our gaze on the promises of God. Javier and Feliciano have passed through death and will never again mourn or cry or hurt. They have overcome. They are sons of God. And even if my sluggish heart lags behind, this truth is worth rejoicing!

Ellie and Feliciano 2008

July 18, 2011

Any clown knows exercise is good for you and too much sugar is bad. Luci, however, is passionate that children understand these truths and put them into practice in their lives. So, for the first time since she was born, this clown put on workout clothes instead of one of her frilly dresses. She joined a teenage youth group and scores of local kids in various forms of exercise: jumping rope, hula hooping, baseball, badminton, calisthenics and running.

"Whoever can come up with the most creative form of exercise will win a ticket!"

This started a hilarious train of gymnastics, a teenage boy who managed to run while twirling a hula hoop around his ankle, a girl who alternately crisscrossed then opened her arms while jumping rope, and my personal favorite, a young boy who twirled a hula hoop around his neck (okay, maybe not the safety award winner, but very amusing!)

"If you drink just one twelve-ounce can of soda a day, at the end of one year, how many kilos of sugar do you think you will have consumed?" Luci asked the audience.

She waved a can of Coke up high so the mothers sitting apart on benches could see. Mexico led the world in Diabetes and obesity, so it was a lesson both generations desperately needed.

"I need sixteen volunteers to fill these bags to the line with dirt!"

The kids rushed to complete the task then ran back and dropped the bags in front of me.

"Sixteen is right! If you drink just one can of soda a day, and I know some of you drink more than that, at the end of a year you will have consumed sixteen kilos of sugar! Look at it!"

The sixteen bags of dirt representing the quantity of sugar consumed impressed the crowd. I looked at one church member who had just been diagnosed with Diabetes and she made a guilty face. She drank more than one soda per day.

"I cut down since the health fair!" she cried.

Then we gave out back packs full of seven kilograms of dirt to each of five children. This was the amount of weight a person could expect to gain as a result of that soda consumption. Luci led these participants and their burdens on a slight jog.

"How do you feel?" she asked after a few minutes.

"Tired!" they yelled.

"How does that extra weight feel?"

"Heavy!"

"How do you think you'd feel carrying that weight around all the time?"

"What diseases do you think you might get because of it?"

"Heart Disease!" "Diabetes!" "Cancer!"

They guessed correctly. They had the knowledge, yet at least five children asked me if they could have the Coke. It's a process.

A youth group had come down from California and was leading a Vacation Bible School at our church in Colonet. They demonstrated two things that move my heart about teenagers:

1. That adolescents who seek God's will for their lives are amazing people. They are focused and confident and the Holy Spirit shapes their dreams.

2. They are the most effective ministers for children. Kids admire them, therefore teens who show that being Christian is "cool," are powerful witnesses for the young.

The team from New Life Christian Church led the children in evangelical crafts, worship, and bible stories but as always with the Lord, the most important outcome was relationship. The visiting teens loved the children and the poverty here broke their hearts. Many told me they wanted to stay.

"A lot of visitors say that," I told them, "but forget when they re-enter their normal lives. I hope you are different! Even if God doesn't call you to come back, remember! Pray for missionaries and support them! Pray for the children you fell in love with! Most of all, know that your work and your compassion were loaves and fishes which God will multiply to produce great yield beyond your knowledge!"

If there is one thing, common in Mexico, that I abhor, it's piñatas. They are not only terrible for children; they symbolize everything that's wrong with charity-based ministries. The donors' gifts are lifted up, a golden calf high above the reach of the common people. The children, or the poor, are blindfolded and spun around, which gets them off balance. Persistent charity likewise, robs the local people of vision and being aware of their own resources. They flail wildly for whatever riches the outsiders bring and when it is showered down upon them, they trample their own brothers and sisters to grab anything they can.

A piñata's usually filled with sugary treats which in the long run, cause harm. And charitable ministries, no matter what they offer, destroy opportunities for the poor to develop skills, build up their own community, help themselves and others, or feel satisfaction.

Fortunately, our group had agreed to fill their piñatas more than halfway with non-sugar items: pencils, stickers, toys. (Still enough to dampen my one soda a day lesson!)

We are all learning. I learned I can still out hula-hoop any child or teenager. That I never want another piñata in our church. That teens living for Christ offer great hope to the world. And no matter what we did right or wrong, the Bible assures us what's most important:
"Love covers over a multitude of sins."
This, the greatest of all, we definitely had!

Luci and Kids Hula-hooping

Carrying 7 Kg Backpacks

August 3, 2011

God loves to play connect-the-dots! Years ago, before Christ, I enjoyed going south of the border to eat lobster and drink Tequila. By way of this first, albeit, unholy dot, a deep love for the country and people of Mexico took hold of me.

In the eighties, my passion became physical exercise and a healthy diet. Working three twelve-hour shifts in ICU gave me four free days a week. I lifted weights in the morning, ran on the beach at midday and taught aerobics in the afternoon. Dot two.

Dot three - In 2002, God gave me a desire to do mission and I began going to the orphanage with Dr. Arnie every month. This world health expert mentored me as to the best way to do healthcare ministry. In June of this year, he came down to instruct and help us put on a Holistic Health Fair. As a result of that event, and in the "CHE" fashion of asking what the community wants, we started a diet and exercise class held at our church in Colonet.

"This class is going to be holistic," I told everyone the first night. "We are learning to care for our temple of God! It will involve knowledge, discipline, emotions, and relationship with ourselves, others and God. We'll learn together, exercise together, encourage and pray for each other, and honor God in it all. How's that sound?"

They were excited to learn and to lose weight. Not surprisingly, the baseline height, weight and Body Mass Index we did on each participant showed nine obese, two overweight and one within the normal range, which was me, the gringa teacher.

"We want to be Barbies!" they joked.

For the first week's exercise, we walked the outskirts of the neighborhood. The next week someone suggested we go to the park, where some walked and some ran. The third week, they wanted music. Here God connected the dots of my life. Decades later, without the lobster and Tequila, I was living and serving in Mexico and about to teach my first aerobics class in three decades. To lift up sisters in this way, to give them the power to change their lives, all the while depending on and glorifying God, I couldn't have designed a more perfect ministry for myself! Yet God knew, back when I was downing Margaritas, that one day, I would enjoy the far greater pleasure, the only real pleasure in this life – that which comes from doing His will!

***

"These might not be appropriate," I told Enrique.

I was going through the songs on *Aretha Franklin's Greatest Hits* and *Flashdance,* two of my old favorites for doing aerobics. The lyrics of "Dr. Feelgood" were questionable but when "Seduce Me Tonight" came on, the Holy Spirit told me, "Definitely not!" I settled on various gospel hits sung by Etta James, not exactly Mexican, but lively.

We had a ball, dancing in the dirt lot outside the church under a pink twilit sky. Then we did stretches on blankets and closed, as always, in prayer.

"You know how to cook healthy! We don't!" Anel said. "Give us some recipes!"

"Okay," I answered. "I will! Meantime, cut way down on the sugar and use a tenth of the oil!" (Here, they float the food they're frying, a sight which horrifies me almost as much as watching a two year-old chew gum!)

It's a holistic ministry, incorporating body, mind and spirit, and best of all, it's relational. We look like just a bunch of women having fun, but if you look harder, you'll see we are growing in love for each other and for our Maker.

"Do you not know that your body is a temple of the Holy Spirit, who is in you, whom you have received from God? ...Therefore honor God with your body."
(1 Cor. 6:19&20)

Sit-ups In The Park

Exercise Is Fun!

September 12, 2011

It has been a month since I sat down in the study nook of our bedroom to write. My dusty little desk showed the neglect.

In August Enrique and I drove to the Sonoran desert, Mexico's Sahara, for fellowship and training with regional leaders of Community Health Evangelism. We are glad to have been accepted for service in Global CHE Enterprises, a non-profit agency headed by Dr. Hugo Gomez, a Guatemalan physician who has led and taught CHE ministries for over twenty years. (See globalche.org)

Then I was on to Pasadena for the West Coast Healthcare Missions Conference. Here the most brilliant minds in international healthcare mission spoke of what we've done wrong – through charity and drug-based ministries – and what we're learning is better – to empower communities toward their own transformation to health. The doctors, pastors, and missionaries who spoke showed us: there are as many ways to empower communities toward physical, emotional and spiritual health as there are willing, thinking, servants of God.

I flew twice the next week, first into my husband's arms for three short days then to Boston without him since my country refused to let him in. Dad's ninetieth birthday celebration was wonderful, with our large loud family and a few friends he's had for eighty years!

Ten days later, Enrique picked me up at the border and finally, I got to go home. But with the huge power outage, our small town had vanished.

"Looks like Jesus came back!" said Enrique.

Without a single light shining, indeed, the whole village might have been raptured. Our little solar-powered lights still shone about the mission base, however, and once inside, we lit a candle and gave much thanks to be home.

Our partners, Kathy Wilson and Doug and Linda Petit, have moved in, parking their large RVs in the base. They intend to stay some months and help with the implementation of Community Health Evangelism in Colonet.

I went to work immediately, teaching at a purity conference for teenage girls Saturday and Sunday. Working alongside other Christians with the desire to show God's love and teach His best practices for their precious lives gave me the knowledge that I was truly home!

October 5, 2011

On an early morning run, Enrique and I approached a small white building with a cement block out front. A large hook hung from a wood frame over a pit of boiling water. It was the only structure in sight, all else was fields and farmlands.

"They sacrifice animals there," he told me.

Indeed, the carcass of a huge pig lay on the cement. Blood poured out of its deep throat wound and the upper body had already been skinned.

Helter skelter dark thoughts ran through my mind.

"What are you saying? Sacrifice for what?"

"To sell the meat, Ellie. What do you think?"

Our communication glitch occurred because the word *sacrificar* in Spanish can refer to either religious sacrifice or butchering for market, so Enrique had said "sacrifice" when he meant "butcher." Though it didn't much matter to the swine, *I* was relieved that he'd been killed for *carnitas* rather than devil worship.

Thanks be to Jesus, the days are past when God required blood sacrifices to atone for man's sins. How pleasant that instead of slitting a lamb's throat, I can reconcile myself to Him in early morning prayer! Yes, Lord!

Yet, we are called to offer our bodies, our entire lives as living sacrifices. (Romans 12:1) The sign at the slaughterhouse reads *"Sala de Matanza Navarez."* That means "Navarez's Slaughterhouse" but if you translated it literally it would read, "Killing Rooms of Navarez." Everyday God arranges personalized "killing rooms" for each of us. Various opportunities come to us where we can to choose His will over ours, show His unconditional love rather than our own judgmental heart. These are the "killing rooms" of our flesh where we can "offer our bodies as living sacrifices."

Sometimes, though, it would be easier to slaughter a few goats than to put aside worry, to sacrifice a couple of doves rather than forgive people who've hurt me. Even to kill and burn a cow would be simpler than continuous obedience to the guidance of the Holy Spirit! But these ceremonial sacrifices don't change hearts, and the heart is always what matters to God.

And my heart has been anxious. Even though the Lord has brought the other members of our team to help, my "to do" list looms over me like a stone tower about to fall. I know He wants me to let Him use these circumstances to bring me to a deeper level of trust, to recognize my puniness and lean into His strength. So in the middle of the night, when my list won't let me fall back to sleep, I go to my chair.

"Abba! Father!" I cry out.

The battle begins. I reel in my mind as many times as needed until I recognize that there is no thought worth thinking. Then He stills my soul; He shows me great and wonderful things, and I give Him permission to go on molding me.

As living sacrifices, we crawl on and off the altar, but slowly we grow more willing and our Father is merciful and patient. How exciting, then, when shoots of godliness, depths of faith and character, peace that surpasses understanding, sprout up like Kathy's little seedlings, holding equal promise! The wonderful dance between our perseverance and His grace.

"They go from strength to strength,
till each appears before God in Zion."
(Psalm 84:7)

October 24, 2011

"I have to be at two meetings in Vicente Guerrero on Saturday, so I don't know if I can open the gate."

The Director of the elementary school told us this as casually as if he were saying he might be five minutes late. This was not a problem of language; we understood perfectly what he was saying. Thirty volunteers had toiled for weeks, planning and preparing every detail of a Health Fair designed for two-hundred and twenty children, and it might not happen because he couldn't swing by and unlock the schoolyard.

Blank face, flabbergasted, I managed only to blurt out, "Could you find someone else?" With great restraint I did not add, "Duh!"

He answered, "Maybe."

God has been teaching me my utter helplessness without Him. This was the final exam. I passed only because it was not multiple choice; there was just one answer – pray and depend on the Lord for everything.

And of course, He came through. A member of the school committee opened the gate. (She didn't have the key for the bathrooms but we couldn't be bothered by details!)

Lots of friends came from the orphanage (*FFHM.org*) to help. Joy and Ciry, two nurses with huge hearts, worked with women from the church registering, weighing and measuring each child for BMI. A great group of teens set up their teaching stations using self-designed posters and fun participatory-style lessons. They had attended two training sessions, mastered their assigned lessons, and served with absolute grace. Flawless behavior from teens? Surely a gift from God!

"Only children whose mothers are here can be scheduled for the dentist tomorrow, "Aida told us. "The rest need to have appointments later in the week so we can notify the parents."

Tales of A Five-Star Missionary

The two dentists, Aida and Laura, examined every mouth while Sandra, a hygienist, taught the waiting children oral care.

"Who knows what germs are?" Gloria, one teen teacher asked.

She and Maite used colored glitter to represent the microbes we pass to others when we don't wash our hands. A big cough produced a handful of red glitter germs which spread quickly as she shook hands with the children at her booth. After several washed their hands in a bowl of still water, the kids could see the "colonies" of germs that stayed behind, as opposed to those that "washed away" when they used running water.

"Di No!" was a favorite. Kids threw bean bags to knock down a pyramid of plastic sand-filled containers. Each was labeled with something to which they should "Say No!" - gossip, drugs, smoking, violence, alcohol, and more.

Luci the clown taught her favorite - the harm of excess sugar consumption. Kids measured out the twelve teaspoons of sugar each can of Coke contains then put on backpacks filled with seven kilograms of dirt. That equaled the quantity of weight they could gain by drinking just one can of soda a day for one year.

After a few minutes of running behind the clown or imitating her calisthenics, most yelled out, *"Cansado!"* (tired!) or *"Pesado!"* (heavy!) when asked how they felt. The point was so they could feel what it's like to carry around extra kilos and to think what harm and diseases could come to their bodies. However, some of the older boys would finish the exercise and boast, "I'm not tired!" Then Luci, not wanting the lesson to fail, would lead them in another round of calisthenics until they admitted defeat. As the midday sun stole the shade, however, the aging clown's aerobics got noticeably less vigorous!

***

"Come on, little baby, jump!"

Dr. Heb, Uriel, and Chuy led the exercise station. When a tiny girl made her way toward the jump rope area, everyone cheered her on. The precious toddler, wearing a huge smile, lifted her feet over the grounded rope and received a huge round of applause!

Doug, Kathy, Linda, Enrique, Gene, and many locals did crowd control, fed the volunteers, and moved groups of five children from station to station. The local doctor spoke to moms about nutrition. Dr. Janet, twenty-three and assigned to this lonely outpost, has few friends or forms of recreation. We invited her to church and she attended not only Sunday service but joined our Nutrition and Exercise class Monday night. Now if we can just get her to exchange her four-inch stilettos for Reeboks!

"Se vale!" they say in Mexico, which means, "It's worth it!"

Without a doubt, the Health Fair for Children was worth every drop of sweat and brainpower. However, the real value will be in how God uses it to advance our way into the community, an important stage of "Community Health Evangelism."

People look older than their age here. Poor diet, hard work in sun and wind weather their faces and skin. The real toll, though, comes from lack of hope. This is what ages them and leaves their stares blank. Yet, hope still lights up their children's eyes, and that tells me we are not too late.

Please pray for the follow-up with parents in the park Wednesday evening, for the opening of hearts and minds to the promise of abundant life!

Trying Fruits and Veggies

Junior Athlete

Recyclers!

Glitter Germs!

Kids With Backpacks Follow The Clown

October 29, 2011

The invitation had been, "Come to the park in Colonet on Wednesday evening to learn the results of the Children's Health Fair!" We started with the bad news.

"Mexico passed the United States last year; they are now number one in the world for obesity and Diabetes! Diseases that, before, were only seen in adults, are now affecting your children – high blood pressure, Diabetes, elevated cholesterol! Mothers, I know you love your children and want to give them treats, but too much soda and sweets ruin their teeth and cause many health problems!"

The local doctor, a visiting dentist, Aida, and Sandra, her assistant, also spoke on the importance of prevention. We taught "The Three Things" a person can do to prevent eighty percent of Heart Disease and Diabetes and forty percent of Cancer. (Do you know what they are? If not, check out hepfdc.org)

Then the Holy Spirit turned the conversation holistic.

"Hermanos, we're missionaries; God has called each of us to serve in Mexico and has poured His love for you into our hearts! We see that life is hard here; stress and poverty can cause many problems – physical, emotional, and spiritual."

Some smiled warmly at the mention of love, others just listened.

"We didn't come to give away clothes or food! Many ministries give, give, give - clothes, food, houses, and nothing really changes!"

Some older women nodded; having seen a flood of donations come down from the North.

"We have a different vision! We want to work with you, the local people, to train volunteers who can then teach their neighbors: how to prevent disease, how to have peace with God, and to work together to find solutions for community problems! As a gringa who grew up far away, I don't know the same things you know! Only you can decide what are the biggest problems, but we can help you find what resources are already here to solve them. Maybe one day I'll go back to the United States! You can't depend on me or any other outsider to fix your problems! All we want is to come alongside you, to empower you to lift up Colonet, out of poverty!"

Already one grandmother was listing the major troubles, "Illness, trash, disputes with neighbors..."

With a few actresses from the audience, we performed the "River Crossing" drama, an introductory lesson to Community Health Evangelism. I, a foreign missionary, stood next to a local woman at the bank of a swollen river, marked by blue tape on the concrete floor.

"How can we cross?" she asked. "It's too high!"

"I know the way," I assured her.

She was scared but I carried her on my back, stepping on small scatter rugs which represented rocks. Soon, however, I grew too tired from the burden, and dropped her on an "island" then went back for two others waiting to cross.

"No, I'm too tired!" I complained. "No more carrying!"

"But we don't know how and we're afraid!"

Finally, with encouragement, they followed me, learning to cross on the rocks and meeting with success. The missionary left suddenly and went back to the U. S. but those who had learned went back to help the one stranded on the island.

"What did you see?" we asked.

"You taught us what you knew so we could do it ourselves!" one answered.

Another said, "It's just what you were telling us! If we learn how to do something, we can teach others!"

I held the woman's face in my hands and told her, "I could kiss you!"

We were laughing and enjoying the fun, but the night was charged by intensity and promise. The first phase of Community Health Evangelism, "Entering the Community," is complete. Our "Nutrition and Exercise" class is drawing women from the community, people we met through the Health Fair show promise as CHE leaders, and "peace with God and neighbors" is a goal we all yearn for.

"For I know the plans I have for you," declares the Lord, "plans to prosper you and not to harm you, plans to give you hope and a future."
(Jeremiah 29:11)

Crossing The River

Tales of A Five-Star Missionary

December 2, 2011

Therapist Judy Perry, in her Purity Conferences for teenagers, advises young women to "keep their gift wrapped" until marriage. Invited to speak in schools and on Christian radio here in the Baja, she's tackled the difficult topics of sexual abuse and the importance of sexual purity before marriage. During one week-long visit, I accompanied her everywhere she taught or spoke, lapping up her wisdom.

"You can do it, Ellie! I'll give you material to read and Spanish hand-outs. Add your own story and your love for the girls, and that's the program! Believe me, the girls here need to hear this!"

A disturbed man once trampled my heart for a period of three years. The verbal and emotional abuse he'd unleashed was the most destructive thing that ever happened to me. Our amazing Redeemer-God had used the experience to give me His heart for women in such relationships. My passion was first of all, to make them aware. Abuse was so prevalent among the indigenous poor, I told many sisters, "If all your neighbors are eating poisonous snakes, you might not know there's a better diet!"

Our core clinic staff, Nora, Angelina, and I, had counseled, taught, and prayed done spiritual battle for many dear ladies whose souls were more wounded than their bodies.

I had decided to do my first Purity Conference to those most dear to me - the disabled teenage girls from the orphanage.

Mary Kos, the director of the Learning Center, responded to the idea of a sleepover with enthusiasm.

"Of course! The kids would love it! They miss you!"

Women from my home church, Solana Beach Presbyterian, bought Teddy Bears – brown, blue, in a gown, huge, small and cuddly – a different one for each girl's bunk.

"Hi Ellie! How are you?"

The group, aged twelve to fifteen, arrived Friday afternoon, eager to show off their new language skills. Most of them had been attendants in my wedding, immature children who spoke only Spanish. Who, then, were these mature bilingual teenagers? Alexis' voice had deepened to that of a man's, but gladly, he had not lost his belly laugh or rib-breaking hugs. Zaida, who shed her walker for my wedding, had gripped Dirk's hand that day and limped unsurely down the aisle. This same girl, now twelve, walked alone, even ran, her inner strength and balance as noticeable as the physical.

"They're so grown up!" I exclaimed to Mary.

She beamed like a proud mother, responding, "Yes, and such good kids!"

We started by reading a Spanish translation of Max Lucado's book, *You Are Special.*

"The Wemmicks were little people made of wood," I read.

They went around putting stickers on each other, grey dots when they said or did something foolish or if their paint had chipped, and gold stars if they displayed talent, intelligence or physical beauty. Puchinello, the main character, was covered in grey dots and felt discouraged until he went to visit Eli, the "Maker" all the Wemmicks.

The great Artisan told him, "Dots and stars only stick to you if you let them! The most important thing is that you trust in my Love, and quit worrying about your stickers!"

Later, He told Puchinello, "Remember, you are special to me because I made you, and I don't make mistakes!"

Every child listening had either a mental or physical disability.

"Have any of you ever received a grey dot? I have. When I was your age, I was soooo skinny, and wore thick glasses and braces. Boys used to tease me, saying, 'Hey, Goolkasian! Do you have to run around in the shower to get wet?' They called me 'Four Eyes' and 'Brace Face!' I felt the burning in my face and knew it was red and that embarrassed me even more!"

These girls had so much compassion! Though they smiled, they didn't laugh – the warmth in their eyes showing they understood the loneliness of rejection. They wrote down their own grey dots and then we threw them away like the trash they were.

The next session, we kept the girls and sent the boys with teachers Ken and Austin.

"Did you ever realize that you are a gift? Actually, a bunch of gifts in one unique package, designed by God! Some of your gifts are to share with everyone: your laughter, your compassion, your intelligence..."

To demonstrate, I opened a series of red and green boxes, revealing smaller and smaller boxes inside each one.

"There's one gift, though, that God designed only for your husband. You should not share this special gift with anyone else!"

Then we talked about unwanted pregnancy, abandonment, abuse, and sexually-transmitted diseases, no light stuff! Yet they listened because they knew all the adults in the room loved them. Linda, a labor and delivery nurse, spoke about disheartened girls going into labor alone. Kathy lightened things up by showing pictures of her daughter's wedding.

"She and her husband both had decided to wait to have sex until they got married. It wasn't easy; they had to take precautions, avoid situations where they could be tempted, have friends to whom they were accountable, but now they have a strong marriage and testimony! They honored the Lord with their bodies and He blessed them!"

We emphasized that it was not necessary to get married to live a fruitful life.

"Look at Juanita!"

One of their teachers, paraplegic from an auto accident, was a great role model and dearly loved.

"Who thinks Juanita has an important life? She's an excellent teacher; she's intelligent, compassionate, and very strong Christian! Amen?"

This woman had impacted each of their lives. The girls gave knowing smiles and nodded their agreement.

"However, it's also possible for people in wheelchairs to get married and have families! I know a woman, Renee Bondi, who is paralyzed from the chest down. She's married, has a son, and gives concerts all over the world with her own Christian songs and testimony!"

"So how many of you today would like to promise the Lord you'll stay virgin until marriage?"

Every girl raised her hand. We passed out pens and booklets.

"I'm not going to tell you what to write and no one else will read it. So say whatever you want and keep it; put it away somewhere in your house! It's between you and Jesus!"

Oh, with such thought they began to compose their letters! Some ripped up the first and started another. Some wrote furiously, others slowly. Only Fernanda, the youngest, did nothing. Debra, her teacher, went and sat beside her and they talked back and forth.

She must not want to do it, I thought, but later Debra set me straight.

"Fernanda doesn't know how to write! She asked me what to do because she wanted to promise God but couldn't write a letter! We thought about it, came up with the idea of a word picture, and she went right to work!"

They put their promises in their backpacks and the class was finished. We lit a bonfire, made *smores*, and sang praise songs to our Maker. In many ways, "disabled" was a grey dot I'd never apply to these special children. Each one was special to God and truly, He never makes a mistake.

> *"For you created my inmost being;*
> *you knit me together in my mother's womb.*
> *I praise you because I am fearfully and wonderfully made;*
> *Your works are wonderful,*
> *I know that full well."*
> (Psalm 139:13-14)

Reading *You Are Special*

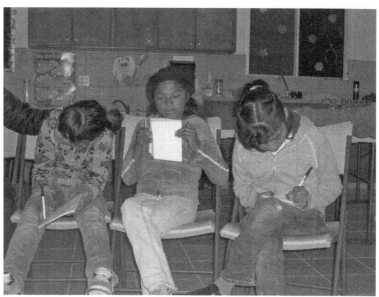
Fernanda, Zaida, and Brenda Writing Their Letters

We Love Our Bears!

Christmas, 2011

Children feel the "magic" of Christmas, that special quality that goes far beyond presents and snowflakes. Adults often miss it. Shopping, wrapping, decorating, cooking, visits and parties prevent stillness, wherein exists the essence of the season. Stillness brings wonder, which Webster's defines as "rapt attention or astonishment at something awesomely mysterious or new to one's experience."

That something is holiness. It is awesomely mysterious and new to our experience because it is a divine quality, and when it touches our lives, we marvel. The Bible says, *"Peter and all his companions were 'astonished' at the catch of fish they had taken."* (Luke 5:9)

They knew after fishing all night and catching nothing that Jesus had performed a miracle. We, too, can "fish all night" and never "catch" holiness. How many times have I prayed, done ministry, worshipped in my own strength, out of touch with the Holy Spirit, catching nothing!

When by grace we grasp it, especially within us, we might, like Peter, be awestruck by the vast difference between our smallness and His Perfection.

The disciple cried out, *"Go away from me, Lord; I am a sinful man!"*

Isaiah the Prophet also cried, *"Woe to me! I am ruined!"* when he saw *"the King, the Lord Almighty."* (Isaiah 6:5)

In both instances God rushed to comfort them.

He told Peter, *"Don't be afraid!"* and touched Isaiah's lips with a live coal to atone for his sins.

Like Peter, my failings are so visible. After four years as a missionary, I still whine when the hot water goes out in the middle of a shower, a tarantula settles on my kitchen counter, or the month's donations don't cover our expenses. Yet my greatest fear is that I'm not growing as a Christian, evidenced by angry outbursts at my husband, frustration in ministry, and looking back so often to the comforts of San Diego that God may yet turn me into a pillar of salt!

My husband, wonderful pastor that he is, applies the word of God to my wounds.

"Ellie, everything is okay! You think God doesn't understand you? He made you five-star and now you're living two-star! Why? Because you love living in mud and dirt and being woken up by roosters or alcoholic neighbors? No! You're here to serve God! All you have to do is keep loving and trusting! The rest is up to Him!"

That lessens my fear. The Bible and personal experience both tell me, *"there is no one righteous, not one."* (Romans 3:10) In the deepest part of myself and others, impurity still breathes. All our prayers, our earnest longings to be godly, don't make us so. If anyone had told me, after four years as a missionary, that I would still struggle with the same sins, the same fleshly desires, the same – well - *self*, I would have thought him crazy. *I'll be very holy by then,* I would have thought but not said out loud.

But I'm not holy, except in moments when grace has its way. Yet if I look deeply, beyond my inadequate sinful self, I find the baby Jesus, His luminescence shining in my darkness. His grace - the live coal that sears my soul and takes away my guilt - His grace tells me, *"Don't be afraid!"* And with that divine assurance, I can enter holiness with hope, not fear.

To enter holiness is not to become it. Sometimes, because ego and all its selfish desires are visiting, the harsh message to God is, "There's no room for you!"

Then Jesus is born in another place. Other times, through prayer and obedience, I consent to make room for divine will. Then Jesus is born in me, not once as in salvation, but more and more often as I grow in wisdom.

His holiness empowers me to act as He would act, to love as He would love, to forgive, heal, speak Truth and be Light. Through Him I can choose peace over the violence in my heart, forgiveness over division, and righteousness over sin. Through Him, I can also choose Jaramillo over La Jolla and two-stars over five.

Christ has been born; those who receive Him receive eternal life. But until we are like Him, until we see Him face to face, we must daily choose His holiness over our fickle hearts! I long to be like Mary, who responded to the divine plan for her life by saying,

"May it be to me as you have said."
(Luke 1:38)

When I've tried so hard to be saintly, but people or circumstances blindside me and I lay wounded, ineffective, and confused, then God waits. He waits for me to say, not "Why?" or "What next?" but, *"May it be to me as you have said!"*

With that attitude of surrender, His life in me grows stronger. Still, it's a daily choice. You, my friends - your support, your prayers and encouragement -are the strength I use to choose wisely. Merry Christmas! I love you!

About The Author

Ellie Goolkasian Lugo is a missionary nurse in the Baja California, Mexico. She worked thirty-eight years for hospitals, surgery centers, Intensive Care Units, and Hospice. In 2007, responding to a distinct call of God, she left a comfortable life and job in San Diego's North County and began a new life serving the poor.

As a writer she felt God's call to share her most intimate experiences with humor and reflection. Ellie's stories welcome the reader deeply into the lives of both missionaries and indigenous farmworkers of the Baja. The tales went out as letters to her friends and supporters who then encouraged her to compile them into a book. *Tales of A Five-Star Missionary* won first place in the San Diego Christian Writers Guild 2012 Writing Awards for the "Best Unpublished Manuscript" and stimulated her to move it out of that category!

She lives with her husband, Pastor Enrique Lugo, in Jaramillo, Mexico. They are hosts of a missionary base and pastors of the "Unidos En Cristo" Christian church. Ellie's ministry goal is to empower people through healthy spiritual and physical practices.

You can sign up for her stories by email at goolklugo@gmail.com or wait for her next book.

Made in the USA
San Bernardino, CA
27 March 2015